This Republic

This Republic

ILLUMINATING REPUBLICAN GOVERNMENT

Will Butts

Liberty's Lamp Books
QUINCY, MA

Copyright © 2014 by Will Butts.

Printed in the United States of America

All rights reserved. No part of this publication may be reproduced, distributed or transmitted in any form or by any means, including photocopying, recording, or other electronic or mechanical methods, without the prior written permission of the publisher, except in the case of brief quotations embodied in critical reviews and certain other noncommercial uses permitted by copyright law. For permission requests, write to the publisher, addressed "Attention: Permissions Coordinator," at the address below.

Cover Design by LLPix Designs
www.LLPix.com

Cover painting: John Adams by John Singleton Copley, 1783

Liberty's Lamp Books
377 Willard Street #338
Quincy, MA 02169
www.libertyslampbooks.com

Book Layout ©2013 BookDesignTemplates.com

Library of Congress Cataloging-in-Publication Data

ISBN 978-0-9911175-0-5

This Republic. Illuminating Republican Government / by Will Butts

Contents

Chapter One: What is a Republic?
The Framework of Republican Government

Chapter Two: Why a Republic?
The Best Form of Government

Chapter Three: A Free, Democratic Republic
The Consent of the Governed

Chapter Four: A Mixed Republic
The One, the Few, and the Many in the Legislature

Chapter Five: A Balanced Republic
Separating the Legislative, Executive, and Judicial Powers

Chapter Six: This Republic
Preserving the Public Liberty

Appendix I: Thoughts on Government — *John Adams*

Appendix II: The Constitution of the United States

Appendix III: For Further Reading

For the American People...

The preservation of liberty depends upon the intellectual and moral character of the people. As long as knowledge and virtue are diffused generally among the body of a nation, it is impossible they should be enslaved.

— John Adams

CHAPTER 1

What is a Republic?
The Framework of Republican Government

When the American republic was founded, it was just the latest in a long line of republican governments extending back to ancient times. From the Hebrew Commonwealth of the Bible; to Athens, Carthage, and Rome; to Venice, Geneva, the Netherlands; and even to the Kingdom of England, republican governments have spanned the centuries. But what exactly is this system of government? What was it the American founders endeavored to create? What is a republic?

To John Adams, a republic was "an empire of laws and not of men."[1] To James Madison, a republic was "a government which derives all its powers directly or indirectly from the great body of the people, and is administered by persons holding their office during pleasure, for a limited period, or during good behavior."[2] And to Roger Sherman, a republic was:

> A government under the authority of the people, consisting of legislative, executive, and judiciary powers; the legislative powers vested in an assembly, consisting of one or more branches, who, together with the executive, are appointed by the people, and dependent on them for continuance, by periodical elections, agreeably to an established constitution; and that what especially denominates it a republic is its dependence on the public or people at large, without any hereditary powers.[3]

The law, the authority of the people, representative government, the balance of powers, and a written constitution: these are principles that characterize a government to be a republic. Yet these principles all stem from a single idea, the republican idea, the idea of the republic, the *res publica*:

> The word *res* ... signified in the Roman language, wealth, riches, property; the word *publicus, quasi populicus*, and *per syncope poplicus*, signified public, common, belonging to the people; *res publica*, therefore, was *publica res*, the wealth, riches, or property of the people.
>
> *Res populi*, and the original meaning of the word republic could be no other than a government in which the property of the people predominated and governed; and it had more relation to property than liberty. It signified a government in which the property of the public, or people, and of every one of them, was secured and protected by law. This idea, indeed, implies liberty

because property cannot be secure unless the man be at liberty to acquire, use, or part with it, at his discretion, and unless he have his personal liberty of life and limb, motion and rest, for that purpose.

It implies, moreover, that the property and the liberty of all men, not merely of a majority, should be safe. For the people, or public, comprehends more than a majority, it comprehends all and every individual; and the property of every citizen is part of the public property, as each citizen is part of the public, people or community. The property, therefore, of every man has a share in government, and is more powerful than any citizen, or party of citizens. It is governed only by the law.[4]

Though republics existed long before Rome, the Latin term for the republican idea remained. *Res publica* translates literally as the public riches, the common wealth, or the property of the people. It translates more loosely as the public matter or the public thing. It is all of the people, all of their property, and all that concerns them, under the law.

For the idea of the *res publica*, or republic, is that the law is supreme; that every person and every thing would be governed, not by men, but by law, by a set of rules that applied to all:

> Others more rationally define a republic to signify only a government in which all men, rich and poor, magistrates and subjects, officers and people, masters and servants, the first citizen and the last, are equally subject to the laws. This, indeed, appears to be the true and only true definition of a republic.[5]

> The republic is the people's affair. But "the people" is not just any collection of human beings gathered together in any sort of way, but the gathering of a large number of people associated by their agreement on the laws for the common good.[6]

The common good, the common wealth, the public riches, the public matter, the public thing, the people's property, and the people's affair: these are all variations of the *res publica*.

For the *res publica* is the law: the "public thing" created for the purpose of securing and protecting all individuals and all property. The law is for the entire public; therefore, it must apply to all, and none must be exempt from it. A government where law applies only to some and not to others would not be republican:

> It may be laid down as a first principle, that neither liberty nor justice can be secured to the individuals of a nation, nor its prosperity promoted, but by a fixed constitution of government, and stated laws, known and obeyed by all.[7]

> The laws, which are the only possible rule, measure, and security of justice, can be sure of protection, for any course of time, in no other form of government: and the very name of a republic implies, that the property of the people should be represented in the legislature, and decide the rule of justice.[8]

A republic is, therefore, a government of laws and not of men, because in a republic, all men are subservient to the law, to the *res publica*, to the common good.

But a republic is something further, for laws do not appear from thin air. Laws must be made; they must be written and enacted. And to make law is to *legislate*, from the Latin *legis*, meaning law or agreement, and *latio*, meaning to propose or bring forth. An individual lawmaker is thus a *legislator*, a bringer of laws, and a body of lawmakers is a *legislature*.

In order to make law, both legislators and legislatures must be vested with lawmaking authority, or *legislative power*. Legislative power is derived from the sovereignty of the people, who entrust the authority to rule them, in those that make the rules:

> In all governments the sovereignty [the ruling authority] is vested in that man or body of men who have the legislative power.
>
> Governments are divided into despotisms, monarchies, and republics. A despotism is a government in which the three divisions of power, the legislative, executive and judicial, are all vested in one man. A monarchy is a government where the legislative and executive are vested in one man, but the judicial in other men ... in despotisms and monarchies, therefore, the legislative authority being in one man, the sovereignty is in one man.
>
> In republics ... the sovereignty, that is, the legislative, is always vested in more than one ... it might be vested in two persons, or in three millions, or in any other intermediate number; and in every such supposable case the government would be a republic.[9]

So a republic, in addition to being a government of laws, is a government where the sovereignty, the lawmaking authority, the legislative power, is vested in more than one person.

The laws in a republic are made, not by a single person, but by an assembly of persons. And whenever two or more people assemble to formulate law, that assembly is a legislature: a gathering of legislators, or lawmakers; a body entrusted with exercising the legislative power:

> By the legislative power we understand the power of *making*, *altering*, or *repealing* laws, which, in all well-ordered governments, hath ever been lodged in a succession of the supreme councils or assemblies of a nation.[10]

Thus, the framework of republican government, the structure at its very foundation, is a government of laws made by more than one person, by a legislature. A republic is a government where the ruling authority of a people, derived from the people themselves and their property, is vested in a legislative assembly to enact the laws for the rest of the public.

* * *

Continuing the line from ancient to modern times, this republican system of government was introduced to America by the English settlers at Jamestown, who in 1619, after over a decade of just trying to survive in the harsh American wilderness, established the first legislature in America:

> The most convenient place we could find to sit in was the choir of the church, where Sir George Yeardley, the governor, being set down in his accustomed place, those of the Council of Estate sat next to him on both [sides], except only the secretary, then appointed speaker, who sat right before him ... all the burgesses took their places in the choir, till a prayer was said ... prayer being ended ... all the burgesses were entreated to retire themselves into the body of the church; which being done, before they were fully admitted, they were called in order and by name, and so every man took the oath of supremacy, and then entered the Assembly.[11]

This account describes a bicameral, or two-house legislature: an upper house of few (a council, or senate) and a lower house of many (an assembly of burgesses, or house of representatives); this legislature, together with a single executive (a governor), fashioned the laws for rest of the colony: a framework of government familiar to this day.

Barely a year after Jamestown, in 1620, republican government continued to take root in America as forty-one men gathered off the coast of what is now Massachusetts, to sign what would be known as the Mayflower Compact:

> Having undertaken for the glory of God, and advancement of the Christian faith and honor of our king and country, a voyage to plant the first colony in the northern parts of Virginia, do by these present, solemnly and mutually, in the presence of God and one of another, covenant and combine ourselves together into a civil body politic, for our better ordering and preservation and furtherance of the ends aforesaid; and by virtue hereof to enact, constitute, and frame such just and

equal laws, ordinances, acts, constitutions, offices from time to time as shall be thought most meet and convenient for the general good of the colony; unto which we promise all due submission and obedience.[12]

Before felling the first tree, the colonists of Plymouth organized themselves into a "civil body politic," a government of laws and not of men. And the stated purpose of the laws and offices yet to be created: the "general good" of the colony; in other words, the *res publica*.

The governments of the first two permanent English settlements on the continent of North America were republican; they were governments of laws enacted by legislatures, assemblies of lawmakers. And these two would be followed by other settlements with similar republican governments.

In time, thirteen of these settlements, thirteen colonies, would unite to form a republican government on a continental scale; a government of laws and not of men; a government where the legislative power is vested in more than one person, in a legislature, in a congress: the government of the United States of America, a republic of republics.

> — And the very name of a republic implies, that the property of the people should be represented in the legislature, and decide the rule of justice.[13]

CHAPTER 2

Why a Republic?
The Best Form of Government

The founders of the United States had a rare opportunity: to actually choose a form of government for themselves and their posterity. And from all the forms of government in history, they chose a republic. But what other choices did they have? What other forms of government were before them? And why were these other forms rejected in favor of a republic?

Let us begin at the beginning. "If men were angels, no government would be necessary," James Madison wrote.[1] But since men are not angels, if a society were to exist without a government, what would it be called?

In a word, it would be anarchy; not anarchy meaning chaos, disorder, and violence, for these are but the results of anarchy, or the actual definition of the word: the absence of governmental authority.

The word anarchy comes from the Greek words *an* meaning no and *archos* meaning ruler; no ruler, no government, thus *an archos*, or anarchy: a state of lawlessness or political disorder; anarchy: rule by none.

As the number of rulers increased, so developed a term to describe that form of government. A step up from rule by none would be rule by one, or *mon archos*, one ruler: monarchy.

Beyond rule by one, naturally would be rule by few, or *oligo archos*: oligarchy. Rule by few is more commonly known by its other name, from *aristo* meaning best and *kratia* meaning state, *aristo kratia*, a state of the best few: aristocracy.

And it follows that if there can be rule by none, rule by one, and rule by few, there must be rule by many. From *demos* meaning people and *kratia* meaning state, a people's state, or popular government, *demos kratia*: democracy:

> Thus monarchy is defined to be "a sovereignty in one," that is to say, all the rights, powers, and authorities of the whole nation, committed in trust to a single man, without limitation or restriction; aristocracy, the same ample and unlimited power, vested in a small number of men; democracy reserves all these rights, prerogatives, and privileges to the whole nation, and every act of its volition must be determined by a vote.[2]

These governments originated quite naturally, by the people deciding to govern themselves or be governed by others:

> Some small numbers of men, living within the precincts of one city, have, as it were, cast into a common stock, the right which they had of governing themselves and children, and by common consent, joining in one body, exercised such power over every single person as seemed beneficial to the whole; and this men call perfect democracy. Others chose rather to be governed by a select number of such as most excelled in wisdom and virtue; and this, according to the signification of the word, was called aristocracy. When one man excelled all others, the government was put into his hands, under the name of monarchy.[3]

The American founders thus had before them: rule by none (anarchy), rule by one (monarchy), rule by the few (aristocracy), rule by the many (democracy), and rule by law (republic). One of these was to be the government of the United States.

Anarchy, being no government at all, was not even considered. And having just separated from Great Britain, the American people would not likely have submitted to rule by one or by a few, so the forms of monarchy and aristocracy were also discarded.

What remained were rule by the many and rule by law: a democracy or a republic. Obviously the founders chose a republic, but why did they reject a democracy? Why would a democracy, or purely democratic government, be an unsuitable choice for the people of the United States?

A democracy is indeed a popular state, or government of the people, but unlike a republican government, where the lawmaking power is vested in a legislature, in a democratic government, the lawmaking power would be vested in the whole people, gathered in one general assembly:

> Democracy [is] sovereignty in the many, that is, in the whole nation, the whole body, assemblage, congregation ... of the whole people. This sovereignty must, in all cases, be exerted or exercised by the whole people assembled together.[4]

> This kind of government cannot be exercised therefore, over a country of any considerable extent; it must be confined to a single city, or at least limited to such bounds as that the people can conveniently assemble, be able to debate, understand the subject submitted to them, and declare their opinion concerning it.[5]

Even at the time of the founding, the United States was an enormous territory. Assembling in one location, all the people of even a single state, not to mention the whole United States, would be impractical, if not impossible:

> If by the people is meant the whole body of a great nation, it should never be forgotten, that they can never act, consult, or reason together, because they cannot march five hundred miles, nor spare the time, nor find a space to meet.[6]

> The people of Virginia, for example, half a million of souls scattered over a territory of two hundred leagues square should ... have no other authority by which to make or execute a law, or judge a cause, but by a vote of the whole people? Where is the plain large enough to hold them; and what are the means, and how long

would be the time, necessary to assemble them together?[7]

A purely democratic government then, the gathering of an entire people in one general assembly, could not reasonably govern a large people or the people of a large territory.

Such a people in such a territory could, however, delegate their lawmaking authority to a much smaller group, representative of the whole: a representative assembly:

> The legislative power should reside in the whole body of the people. But since this is impossible in large states ... it is fit the people should execute by their representatives what they cannot execute by themselves.[8]

> It is, indeed, impossible that ... men ... should, in a great nation and extensive territory, ever assemble in a body to act in concert; and the ancient method of taking the sense of an assembly of citizens in the capital, as in Rome for example, for the sense of all the citizens of a whole republic, or a large empire, was very imperfect, and extremely exposed to corruption; but, since the invention of representative assemblies, much of that objection is removed.[9]

> The great advantage of representatives is their being capable of discussing affairs; for this the people collectively are extremely unfit, which is one of the greatest inconveniencies of a democracy.[10]

Instead of an entire people assembling in one body (a democratic government), only their representatives would assemble, acting in the person and with the authority of the whole (a republican government):

> The two great points of difference between a democracy and a republic are, first, the delegation of the government in the latter, to a small number of citizens elected by the rest: secondly, the greater number of citizens, and greater sphere of country, over which the latter may be extended.[11]

> In a democracy, the people meet and exercise the government in person; in a republic, they assemble and administer it by their representatives and agents. A democracy, consequently, will be confined to a small spot. A republic may be extended over a large region.[12]

Thus a democracy, on practicality alone, would not have been a suitable government for the people of the United States. But beyond the practical reasons, a democracy, or purely democratic government, would have presented a danger to the people, for democracy by definition is rule by the many, that is, by the majority:

> When a number of men, women, and children are simply congregated together ... there is no political authority among them, nor any natural authority ... not one will have any authority over any other. The first "collection" or authority must be a unanimous agreement to form themselves into a nation, people, community, or body politick, and to be governed by the majority of the suffrages or voices.[13]

But while the legislative power in a democracy would, in theory, be vested in the whole people, in reality it would be vested in a mere majority of those present:

> Although the authority is collected into one center, that center is no longer the nation, but the majority of the nation.[13]

And unlike a republic, in a democracy there would be no appeal or recourse available to any in the minority; there would be no law, no courts, nor any ruling authority at all, just one gathering of all the people and the decision of a majority.

Also unlike a republic, in a democracy no members of the ruling majority could be removed from power. For in a republic, a government with a representative assembly, individual lawmakers can be removed and replaced. But when the people simply gather and take a vote, who is to be removed?

Thus, with all liberty and all property subject to a government consisting solely of an assembly of the people and a majority of votes, a purely democratic government, an unlimited majority power, would inevitably consolidate that power over the people. And democracy, rule by the many, rule by the majority, would then descend into an unlimited tyranny, a rule by the mob:

> Democracy signified a government ... of the people at large, forming in assembly the legal absolute sovereign: but as this, above all others, was subject to irregularity,

confusion and absurdity when unchecked by some balancing power lodged in fewer hands, it was called ochlocracy, or mob rule.[14]

For unlike a republic, a government of law, a democracy would be a government of men. And history has shown that governments of men, the simple forms of monarchy, aristocracy, and democracy, degenerate from being good governments, based on virtuous principles and the best of intentions, into bad governments where the people's liberty and property become endangered:

> For monarchy often degenerates into tyranny, aristocracy into oligarchy, and democracy into licentious anarchy and confusion: so that whoever sets up any one of the former three sorts of government, may assure himself it will not be of any long duration; for no precaution will be sufficient to prevent its falling into the other that is analogous to it.[15]

Furthermore:

> Every form of government that is simple, by soon degenerating into that vice that is allied to it, and naturally attends it, must be unstable. For as rust is the natural bane of iron, and worms of wood, by which they are lure to be destroyed, so there is a certain vice implanted by the hand of nature in every simple form of government, and by her ordained to accompany it.[16]

So with good reason the American founders rejected not only monarchy and aristocracy, but also democracy as a form of government for the people of the United States; for a democracy would have been impractical, would not have lasted, and would not have secured the liberty and property of the people:

> The experience of all former ages had shown that of all human governments, democracy was the most unstable, fluctuating and short-lived.[17]
>
> Democracies have ever been spectacles of turbulence and contention; have ever been found incompatible with personal security or the rights of property; and have in general been as short in their lives as they have been violent in their deaths.[18]
>
> A democracy is a volcano which conceals the fiery materials of its own destruction. These will produce an eruption and carry desolation in their way.[19]
>
> Democracy never lasts long. It soon wastes, exhausts, and murders itself. There never was a democracy yet that did not commit suicide.[20]
>
> Democracy will soon degenerate into an anarchy; such an anarchy that every man will do what is right in his own eyes and no man's life or property or reputation or liberty will be secure.[21]

The American founders had before them, all the governments that ever were, or ever would be, and from among these, they chose a republic. Instead of a government that could rule only a small area, they chose a government that could efficiently govern both a large people and a large territory. Instead of a government with unlimited power vested in one, a few, or many, they chose a government where the whole people would be represented in a legislative assembly. And instead of a government of men, they chose a government of law.

For without law there is no liberty, no property, and no security. In a government of men, in a monarchy, an aristocracy or a democracy, the people would be subject to the whims of one, a few, or many; whereas in a republic, all the people — the one, the few, and the many included — would be subject to the law, to a set of rules that governed the whole people, created by the whole people, through their representatives, assembled.

Given the choices before the American founders, the only form of government suitable to govern the people of the United States was a republic, the best form of government, for none but a republic could secure the liberties of the people for the longest period of time.

> — The great question therefore is, what combination of powers in society, or what form of government, will compel the formation of good and equal laws, an impartial execution, and faithful interpretation of them, so that the citizens may constantly enjoy the benefit of them, and be sure of their continuance.[22]

CHAPTER 3

A Free, Democratic Republic

The Consent of the Governed

A republic, a government of laws, is indeed the best form of government to secure and protect the liberties of the people: the public liberty. But in order for the laws to truly govern, the people must willingly obey them, and must have the ability to alter or repeal them when necessary, should any law begin to outlast its usefulness, or more importantly, should any law begin to encroach on the public liberty.

Laws are more likely to be obeyed if they originate from the very people they are created to secure and protect, that is, if the people themselves make the laws or in some way participate in making them; this is civil liberty and self-government:

> Civil liberty [is defined] to be the power of a civil society to govern itself, by its own discretion, or by laws of

its own making, by the majority, in a collective body, or by fair representation.[1]

A people with civil liberty, a people that governs itself, is a free people. And the government of such a people, a government where the people make their own laws, is a free government. For in a free government, the laws are made with the permission of the people, the consent of the people: *the consent of the governed*:

> In every free government, the people must give their assent to the laws by which they are governed. That is the true criterion between a free government and an arbitrary one.[2]

> For what original title can any man or set of men have to govern others, except their own consent? To usurp dominion over a people ... or to grasp at a more extensive power than they are willing to entrust, is to violate that law of nature which gives every man a right to his personal liberty; and can, therefore, confer no obligation to obedience.[3]

> It is the unalienable birthright of every [free man] ... to participate in framing the laws which are to bind him.[4]

In a republic, the laws are made, not by the people themselves, but by a representative assembly, by a legislature. Therefore, if a republic is to be a free government, the people would need to participate in framing the laws, by in some way participating in the legislature.

In a *free* republic, the people participate in the legislature by choosing its members, by choosing the lawmakers;

for by choosing the lawmakers, the people in a free republic choose which laws are made.

Thus, by way of the people's elected representatives in the legislature, the laws in a free republic are granted the consent of the people, the consent of the governed:

> In a free republic, though all the laws are derived from the consent of the people, yet the people do not declare their consent by themselves in person, but by representatives, chosen by them.[5]

But the consent of the people once acquired, must be maintained. If a free republic is to remain free, the people must retain control of the laws by retaining control of the legislature, and their own representatives; the lawmakers must at all times remain answerable to the people:

> There is danger from all men. The only maxim of a free government ought to be to trust no man living with power to endanger the public liberty.[6]

> The liberty of the people depends entirely on the constant and direct communication between them and the legislature, by means of their representatives.[7]

> It is not only most prudent then, but absolutely necessary ... to give the people a legal, constitutional, and peaceable mode of changing [their] rulers, whenever they discover improper principles or dispositions in them.[8]

In order for the people to prevent themselves from becoming under the dominion of their own legislature, and thus their own selected rulers, they must have it within their power to remove and replace any legislators who begin in any way to tread on the public liberty.

The representatives of the people, therefore, must not keep their offices permanently. The membership of the legislature should be frequently changed so that the laws continually reflect, not the will of the elected legislators, but the will of those who elect them:

> In order to prevent those who are vested with authority from becoming oppressors, the people have a right, at such periods and in such manner as they shall establish by their frame of government, to cause their public officers to return to private life, and to fill up vacant places by certain and regular elections.[9]

> Popular elections ... frequently repeated, are the only possible method of forming a free constitution, or of preserving the government of laws from the domination of men, or preserving [the people's] lives, liberties, or properties in security ... when popular elections are given up, liberty and free government are given up.[10]

An elected and frequently changing legislature will continually reflect the will of the people and will also maintain and perpetuate the consent of the governed. And therefore, through such a legislature, a government of laws can maintain its authority over a people, with the willing obedience of them. This is a free government; this is a free republic:

> No laws have any validity or binding force without the consent and approbation of the people, given in the

persons of their representatives, periodically elected by themselves.[11]

> The people ... are not controllable by any other laws than those to which their constitutional representative body have given their consent.[12]

> The right of the people to participate in the legislature is the best security of liberty, and the foundation of all free government.[13]

By choosing their own lawmakers, the people in a free republic choose which laws are made, and thus remain free. But people in republics have not always had the privilege of choosing their own lawmakers, for not all republics have been free republics:

> If the word republic must be used to signify every government in which more than one man has a share, it is true this must be called by that name; but a republic and a free government may be different things.[14]

> Republics have been divided into three species, monarchical, aristocratic, and democratic republics.[15]

A *monarchical* republic is a government where the legislative power is vested in more than one person (in a legislative assembly of one or more branches), and where a perpetual or hereditary individual holds power separate from the legislative power.

A monarchical republic can be considered to be a free republic only if the people themselves in some way participate in the legislature, that is, if the people choose all or at least part of the legislative assembly.

An example of a free, monarchical republic is the government of Great Britain; for though Great Britain has a perpetual or hereditary monarch, its laws are granted the consent of the people, the consent of the governed, by way of the people's elected representatives in its House of Commons.

An *aristocratic* republic is a government where the legislative power is vested in more than one person (in a legislative assembly of one or more branches); where there is no perpetual or hereditary monarch; and where the people themselves choose none of the officers of government, legislative or otherwise.

An aristocratic republic is *never* a free republic because the people in no way participate in the legislature; the people choose no part of the legislative assembly. Thus, in an aristocratic republic, the laws are never granted the consent of the people, the consent of the governed.

A *democratic* republic is a government where the legislative power is vested in more than one person (in a legislative assembly of one or more branches); where there is no perpetual or hereditary monarch; and where the people themselves choose all or at least part of the legislative assembly.

A democratic republic is *always* a free republic, for in a democratic republic, the people participate in the legislature; they choose all or at least part of the legislative assembly. Thus, in a democratic republic, the laws are granted the consent of the people, the consent of the governed.

The United States is neither a monarchical nor an aristocratic republic. The United States has no perpetual or hereditary monarch. Although a single individual holds the executive power, that power is granted for only four years and is limited to eight. Furthermore, in the United States all constitutional officers of government are chosen either directly by the people, or chosen indirectly by those chosen directly, and all can be removed from office by either the people themselves or their representatives.

Thus, the United States is a democratic republic; it is a government where the people actively participate in the legislature, a government where the laws are granted the consent of the people, the consent of the governed. And because the United States is a democratic republic, and all democratic republics are free republics, the United States is also a free republic.

For in a free, democratic republic, the people govern themselves; the laws come from themselves because the lawmakers come from themselves. And to change or repeal the laws, the people need only change the lawmakers; they need only change the membership of the legislature.

> — To a benevolent mind there can be no spectacle presented by any nation more pleasing, more noble, majestic, or august than ... a government in which the executive authority as well as that of all the branches of the legislature, are exercised by citizens selected at regular periods by their neighbors to make and execute laws for the general good.[16]

CHAPTER 4

A Mixed Republic

The One, the Few, and the Many in the Legislature

In a republic, the legislature is the assembly of those entrusted with making the laws. But within the legislature, how would the laws be made? How would the legislature be structured and organized? Would legislators assemble in just one body, or in two bodies, or more? And if several bodies, how would the legislative power be exercised amongst them?

The American founders knew that republics, though more stable than the forms of monarchy, aristocracy, and democracy, were just as susceptible to the forces of corruption and degeneration that historically afflicted these other forms:

> We have gone back to ancient history for models of government and examined the different forms of those republics, which, having been originally formed with

the seeds of their own dissolution, now no longer exist.[1]

Republics without number arose in Italy; whirled upon their axles or single centers; foamed, raged, and burst, like so many waterspouts upon the ocean. They were all alike ill constituted; all alike miserable; and all ended in similar disgrace and despotism.[2]

Since a similar fate could, or eventually would, befall an American republic, John Adams cautioned at the time:

It is of great importance to begin well; misarrangements now made, will have great, extensive and distant consequences.[3]

A political experiment cannot be made in a laboratory, nor determined in a few hours. The operation once begun, runs over whole quarters of the globe, and is not finished in many thousands of years.[4]

We are now employed, how little so ever we may think of it, in making establishments which will affect the happiness of an hundred millions of inhabitants at a time, in a period not very distant.[5]

The American founders therefore thought it paramount to design their republic in a manner that would emulate those republics of the past which most resisted degeneration, and which endured for the longest period. And the design they chose was that of a mixed republic, a republic that incorporated within it, the simple forms of monarchy, aristocracy, and democracy: the one, the few, and the many:

If any measure can tend to preserve this commonwealth, to assure both her liberty and power, and to establish a perpetual union and harmony in all things, the most effectual will be to give the people a share in the government: and the most advantageous thing to us will be, not to have a simple and unmixed form of government; neither a monarchy, an oligarchy, nor a democracy, but a constitution tempered with all of them: for each of these forms, when simple, very easily deviates into abuse and excess; but when all of them are equally mixed, that part which happens to innovate, and to exceed the customary bounds, is always restrained by another that is sober, and adheres to the established order.[6]

The best legislators of all ages agree in this, that the absolute power, which originally is in the whole body, is a trust too great to be committed to any one man or assembly; and therefore, in their several institutions of government, power in the last resort, was always placed by them in balance, among the one, the few, and the many.[7]

An equal mixture of monarchy, aristocracy, and democracy, is the only free government which has been able to manage the greatest heroes and statesmen, the greatest individuals and families, or combination of them, so as to keep them always obedient to the laws.[8]

Because "all independent bodies of men seem naturally to divide into the three powers, of the one, the few, and the many," to establish a government that will be stable and remain so, the powers of the one, the few, and the many ought to be incorporated within it. For otherwise, these powers, being natural, would form anyway, and if not balanced, would tear the government asunder.[9]

John Adams called these powers the three natural "orders," noting that when all three were not present and balanced against each other, governments quickly degenerated:

> The only balance attempted against the ancient kings [the one] was a body of nobles [the few]; and the consequences were perpetual altercations of rebellion and tyranny, and butcheries of thousands upon every revolution from one to the other. When the kings were abolished, the aristocracies tyrannized; and then no balance was attempted but between aristocracy [the few] and democracy [the many]. This, in the nature of things, could be no balance at all, and therefore the pendulum was forever on the swing.[10]

> It appears, from the history of all the ancient republics of Greece, Italy, and Asia Minor, as well as from those that still remain in Switzerland, Italy, and elsewhere, that caprice, instability, turbulence, revolutions, and the alternate prevalence of those two plagues and scourges of mankind, tyranny and anarchy, were the effects of governments without three orders and a balance.[11]

Thus, Adams feared that "without three orders, and an effectual balance between them, in every American constitution, it must be destined to frequent unavoidable revolutions: if they are delayed a few years, they must come, in time."[12] So to avoid or prevent such revolutions, monarchy, aristocracy, and democracy — the one, the few, and the many — would be introduced and mixed into the American republic. But how was this to be done?

In the United States, there were to be no hereditary titles; no monarchs or aristocrats; no kings, queens, or nobles who were entitled to office simply because of the families to which they belonged. "In America, there are different orders of offices, but none of men; out of office all men are of the same species, and of one blood; there is neither a greater nor a lesser nobility."[13]

Monarchy, aristocracy, and democracy would be mixed into the American republic by "dividing the legislature into three branches, making the executive one of them, and independent of the other two."[14]

The legislature, the body entrusted with making the laws, would be divided into three parts: a single executive, a senate, and a house of representatives: the one, the few, and the many.

For though a republic is a government of laws, those laws would still need to be written and administered by men, and as Madison wrote:

> In framing a government which is to be administered by men over men, the great difficulty lies in this: You must first enable the government to control the governed; and in the next place, oblige it to control itself.[15]

By dividing the legislature into three parts, the government would be internally controlled by its own members. Every prospective law, every piece of *legislation*, would need to pass through each of the three parts of the legislature, and necessarily through the one, the few, and the many.

All laws would originate in the legislative assemblies, in either the senate or the house of representatives: with either the few or the many. And whenever the few and the many should both agree on a piece of legislation, it would be sent to the one, to the single executive:

> Every bill which shall have passed the House of Representatives and the Senate, shall, before it becomes a law, be presented to the President. [16]

The executive would therefore act as a third part of the legislature, as a counterweight to the two legislative bodies, for "it is impossible to balance two assemblies, without introducing a third power; one or the other will be most powerful, and whichever it is, it will continually scramble till it gets the whole."[17]

Thus, in a mixed republic, no part of the legislature could enact any law without the involvement of the others; and furthermore, each part of the legislature would have the ability to thwart or negate the actions of either, or both, of the other parts, for "there can be no equal mixture without a negative in each branch of the legislature."[18]

Should the house pass a bill, without the concurrence of the senate, the bill would die. Should the senate pass a bill, without the concurrence of the house, the bill would die. Should the house and senate agree on a bill and send it to the executive, the executive could then veto, or reject the bill and return it to them. And if both house and senate then fail to muster the votes necessary to override the executive's veto, the bill would die:

> Every order, resolution, or vote, to which the concurrence of the senate and house of representatives may be necessary ... shall be presented to the President ... and before the same shall take effect, shall be approved by him, or, being disapproved by him, shall be repassed by two-thirds of the senate and house of representatives.[19]

Structuring the legislature in this way creates a circle of power; each part of the circle can check the power of the other two, and any two can check the power of any one; the result being that "no law can be passed in a passion, nor inconsistent with the constitution."[20]

Thus, the United States came to be a mixed republic, using a formula of government that has balanced the natural orders of mankind since the most ancient times, since at least the Hebrew Commonwealth in the time of Moses:

> The government of the Hebrews, instituted by God, had a judge [a chief magistrate], the great Sanhedrim [a council composed of seventy chosen men], and general assemblies of the people.[21]

> Is this not an illustration of the three organisms of the American Constitution, the President, the Senate, and a popular chamber? [22]

The ancient Greeks, too, used a mixed formula of government in the Lacedemonian Commonwealth, in ancient Sparta, instituted by its lawgiver, Lycurgus:

> Lycurgus concluded that every form of government that is simple, by soon degenerating into that vice that is allied to it, must be unstable. The vice of kingly government is monarchy; that of aristocracy, oligarchy; that of democracy, rage and violence; into which, in process of time, all of them must degenerate. Lycurgus, to avoid these inconveniences, formed his government not of one sort, but united in one all the advantages and properties of the best governments; to the end that no branch of it, by swelling beyond its due bounds, might degenerate into the vice which is congenial to it ... this system preserved the Lacedemonians in liberty longer than any other people.[23]

The government of England, with which the American founders were most familiar, also had a mixed formula of government, consisting of a monarch, a house of lords, and a house of commons: the one, the few, and the many.

The English, in turn, created miniatures of their governmental structure when they colonized America; each colony's government consisted of a governor (a single executive) and a bicameral assembly with an upper house of few and a lower house of many.

And upon separating from Great Britain, the newly formed states followed these examples when creating their own governments. To this day, forty-nine out of the fifty united states have a mixed formula of government consisting of an executive, a senate, and a house of representatives. Nebraska alone varies from this model; its government consists of an executive and a unicameral assembly.

In these and numerous other examples throughout the ages, governments mixed with monarchy, aristocracy, and democracy, or the one, the few, and the many, have proven to be the most stable and enduring known to man.

The American founders, therefore, incorporated this governmental formula into their republic, for they knew that:

> The predominant passion of all men in power ... is the same; that tyranny will be the effect, whoever are the governors, whether the one, the few, or the many, if uncontrolled by equal laws, made by common consent, and supported, protected, and enforced by three different orders of men in equilibrio.[24]

With the legislature in the American republic divided into three independent institutions, an executive, a senate, and a house of representatives, with the powers of the one, the few, and the many balanced against each other, the people could be assured that their republic would endure for the longest period of time.

> — But how are the laws to govern? And how is the equilibrium to be preserved? Like air, oil and water, shaken together in one bottle, and left in repose; the first will rise to the top, the last sink to the bottom, and the second swim between.[25]

CHAPTER 5

A Balanced Republic

Separating the Legislative, Executive and Judicial Powers

In addition to incorporating a balance among the three natural orders — the one, the few, and the many — into their republic, the American founders also incorporated a balance among the three natural powers of the people: that of making laws, that of executing or administering laws, and that of adjudicating laws.

For just as three powers are necessary to balance a legislature, so too are three powers necessary to balance a government:

> Three branches of power have an unalterable foundation in nature ... they exist in every society natural and artificial; and that if all of them are not acknowledged in any constitution of government, it will be found to be imperfect, unstable, and soon enslaved.[1]

> A legislative, an executive, and a judicial power comprehend the whole of what is meant and understood by government. It is by balancing each of these powers against the other two, that the efforts in human nature towards tyranny can alone be checked and restrained, and any degree of freedom preserved in the constitution.[2]

Originally, the government of the United States was not balanced in any way. After separating from Great Britain, the existing Continental Congress wrote the Articles of Confederation, under which was created a single representative assembly, again called a Congress.

This Congress was to be the only government for the whole American people, though it was granted very little power to govern. For after dealing with a monarchy and an over-reaching parliament under Great Britain, the states feared a consolidation of power in one central government.

And the states' fears were justified. For the danger of a government consisting solely of a single assembly is that all the powers of the people — legislation, execution, and adjudication — rest in the same hands, a recipe that quickly leads to despotism and tyranny:

> A single assembly thus constituted, without any counterpoise, balance, or equilibrium, is to have all authority, legislative, executive, and judicial, concentered in it. It is to make a constitution and laws by its own will, execute those laws at its pleasure, and adjudge all controversies, that arise concerning the meaning and application of them, at discretion.[3]

> Since all men are so inclinable to act according to their own wills and interests, in making, expounding, and executing laws, to the prejudice of the people's liberty and security, the sovereign authority, the legislative, executive, and judicial power, can never be safely lodged in one assembly ... because the majority and their leaders, the *principes populi*, will as certainly oppress the minority, and make, expound, and execute laws for their own wealth, power, grandeur, and glory, to the prejudice of the liberty and security of the minority.[4]

To prevent such a consolidation of power and to keep their single-assembly government within its limits, the individual states retained most of the powers of the people within themselves. The Congress under the Articles of Confederation had no executive or judicial powers whatsoever, and only a limited legislative power.

The result of this weak governmental structure, however, was that the legislation passed by the Congress had no teeth. For without an executive to carry out the laws or a judiciary to enforce them, nothing was to stop the states or the people from simply ignoring them.

It therefore proved just as dangerous to the people for a government to have too little power as too much. And within a short period of time, it became apparent that a new form of government was necessary: a central government granted enough power to enact, execute, and enforce its laws.

Thus, the government subsequently created under the Constitution had far more power than its predecessor. But the founders once again faced the question of how to keep the central government from consolidating its power:

> In framing a government which is to be administered by men over men, the great difficulty lies in this: You must first enable the government to control the governed; and in the next place, oblige it to control itself.[5]

A government of divided and balanced powers provided the solution to this problem; the powers granted to a central government were to be separated into different branches and therefore, into different hands; thus, no consolidation of power could occur.

For just as in the mixing of the legislature, separating the powers of the people establishes an internal control within the government. Each power can check the powers of the other two and any two can check any one. This internal control, or circle of power, creates a balance, and this balance preserves liberty:

> Without three divisions of power, stationed to watch each other, and compare each other's conduct with the laws, it will be impossible that the laws should at all times preserve their authority, and govern all men.[6]

Since the laws that govern all men must first be written and enacted, the first division of power is the *legislative* power, the power to make law. And as stated in the previous chapter, the laws were to be made by a *legislature* consisting of the one, the few, and the many: an executive and the two bodies of the *legislative branch*, a senate and a house of representatives.

However, laws once enacted, in and of themselves, mean nothing; they are merely words on paper. Only in their execution are they given life and meaning; thus the need for a second division of power, an *executive* power to *execute*, or carry out the laws:

> The executive power is properly the government; the laws are a dead letter until an administration begins to carry them into execution.[7]

> The executive represents the majesty, persons, wills, and power of the people in the administration of government and dispensing of laws.[8]

And this power of administration, of execution, must be kept separate from the power of lawmaking, of legislation:

> If there is one certain truth to be collected from the history of all ages, it is this: that the people's rights and liberties, and the democratic mixture in a constitution, can never be preserved without a strong executive, or, in other words, without separating the executive power from the legislative.[9]

> The executive represents the people for one purpose, as much as the legislative does for another; and the executive ought to be as distinct and independent of the legislative, as the legislative is of [the executive].[10]

> If the executive power, or any considerable part of it, is left in the hands of either [a senate] or a [house of representatives], it will corrupt the legislature as necessarily as rust corrupts iron, or as arsenic poisons the

human body; and when the legislature is corrupted the people are undone.[11]

For if the same man or body of men holds both the legislative and executive powers, "what is there to restrain them from making tyrannical laws, in order to execute them in a tyrannical manner?"[12]

But if the powers of legislation and execution must be kept separate and distinct, why, as indicated in the previous chapter, should the executive play a role in every piece of legislation? Is this not contradictory?

There is no contradiction because only the legislative branch can actually *legislate*, or write the laws. The executive plays a role only in the enactment of law. He can either accept legislation, or reject it and send it back to the legislative, which can then override the executive if it so chooses. And since the legislative branch has the power to enact law over the objections of the executive, all legislative power rests with the legislative assemblies, leaving none with the executive.

The executive acts as a third branch of the legislature to balance the two legislative assemblies and to check the legislative power if necessary, but that is the extent of any legislative role. The executive's main duty and authority is to exercise the executive power of the people by carrying out the laws that have successfully passed through the legislature.

What of the third division of power? Once the laws have been enacted by the legislature and carried out by the executive, they must be enforced, and any disputes under them resolved: they must be *adjudicated.* This is the responsibility of the *judicial* power. And while the legislative and executive powers need to be kept separate from each other, the judicial power needs to be kept separate from both:

> There is no liberty, if the power of judging be not separated from the legislative and executive powers: were it joined with the legislative, the life and liberty of the citizens would be exposed to arbitrary control; for the judge would then be legislator: were it joined to the executive power, the judge might behave with all the violence of an oppressor.[13]

> Liberty can have nothing to fear from the judiciary alone, but would have everything to fear from its union with either of the other [powers].[14]

> Though individual oppression may now and then proceed from the courts of justice, the general liberty of the people can never be endangered from [them] ... so long as the judiciary remains truly distinct from both the legislative and executive.[14]

Thus, the American founders clearly saw the necessity of separating the natural powers of the people:

> The accumulation of all powers legislative, executive and judicia[l] in the same hands, whether of one, a few, or many, and whether hereditary, self-appointed, or elective, may justly be pronounced the very definition of tyranny.[15]

> There would be an end of every thing were the same man, or the same body ... to exercise those three powers; that of enacting laws, that of executing the public resolutions, and that of judging the crimes or differences of individuals.[16]
>
> But where the executive is in one hand, the legislative in three, and the judicial in hands different from both, there is rarely, if ever, any danger.[17]
>
> Those nations [have] been the happiest who [have] separated the legislative from the executive power, the judicial from both, and divided the legislative power itself into three branches, thereby producing a balance between the legislative and executive authority, a balance between the branches of the legislature and a salutary check upon all these powers in the judicial.[18]

With the natural powers of the people — legislative, executive, and judicial — separated and balanced against each other within the American republic, the people could be assured that no one man or body of men could get hold of all power at once. And thus, the liberties of the people, the public liberty, could be secured and protected for the longest period of time.

> — The legislative department shall never exercise the executive and judicial powers, or either of them; the executive shall never exercise the legislative and judicial powers, or either of them; the judicial shall never exercise the legislative and executive powers, or either of them, to the end it may be a government of laws and not of men.[19]

CHAPTER 6

This Republic

Preserving the Public Liberty

Republican government was instituted in America to preserve liberty. It was instituted first, to transfer the rights and liberties of Englishmen to the American continent. Then, upon the American colonies' separation from Great Britain, republican government was instituted to enshrine those rights and liberties, to which the American people had become accustomed, and for which they had all fought and struggled, into law. And finally, republican government was instituted to transmit those same rights and liberties to posterity, to generations yet unborn.

Republican government begins with the *publica*, with the public, with the people; it begins with the idea that the people are sovereign and that all governmental authority stems from that sovereignty:

> There is but one element of government, and that is, the people. From this element springs all governments.[1]

The *summa potestatis*, the supreme, sovereign, absolute, and uncontrollable power, is placed by God and nature in the people, and they can never divest themselves of it.[2]

All intelligence, all power, all force, all authority, originally, inherently, necessarily, inseparably, and inalienably resides in the people.[3]

And from the people, from the *publica,* is derived the *res publica*: the people's property, the public riches, the common wealth, the common good, the general good, the general welfare; in other words, the public thing: the law.

The law is the set of rules to which all are subject and which all must obey. Laws are the boundaries of a society, of a body politic; they are the covenant between the people and each other:

The body politic is formed by a voluntary association of individuals. It is a social compact, by which the whole people covenants with each citizen, and each citizen with the whole people, that all shall be governed by certain laws for the common good.[4]

Laws exist to secure and protect the liberty and property of the public, of the people, for laws serve to restrain and cage the passions of men. A society without laws, without some governing authority, would be an anarchy:

There can be no uninterrupted enjoyment of liberty, nor any good government, in society, without laws, or where standing laws do not govern ... If the laws were all repealed at once, in any great kingdom, and the event made known suddenly to all, there would scarcely a house remain in possession of its present inhabitant.[5]

Hunger and poverty may make men industrious, but laws only can make them good; for, if men were so of themselves, there would be no occasion for laws.[6]

Laws are intended, not to trust to what men will do, but to guard against what they *may* do.[7]

No man will contend that a nation can be free, that is not governed by fixed laws.[8]

But laws must be made; they must be written and enacted. Then laws must be executed and administered. And finally, laws must be enforced, with any disputes under them resolved. These actions must be carried out in some organized form; thus, government is instituted, as an instrument of the people to establish laws, to maintain order, and to protect and preserve the body politic and the public liberty:

> Government is nothing more than the combined force of society, or the united power of the multitude, for the peace, order, safety, good and happiness of the people.[9]

> The [purpose] of the institution, maintenance, and administration of government is to secure the existence of the body politic; to protect it, and to furnish the individuals who compose it with the power of enjoying, in safety and tranquility, their natural rights and the blessings of life.[10]

> It is the duty of the people, therefore, in framing a Constitution of Government, to provide for an equitable

mode of making laws, as well as for an impartial interpretation and a faithful execution of them, that every man may, at all times, find his security in them.[11]

To enact, execute, and adjudicate laws, power must be placed in men, in one, several, or many men. And for the safety and security of the people and their property, the powers placed in men must be limited and controlled:

> The constant experience of the world has ... proved that nothing intoxicates the human mind so much as power. In the establishment, therefore, of civil government, it would be preposterous to rely on the discretion of any men. A people will never oppress themselves, or invade their own rights; but if they trust the arbitrary will of a body or succession of men, they trust enemies.[12]

> The origin of all civil government, justly established, must be a voluntary compact, between the rulers and the ruled; and must be liable to such limitations, as are necessary for the security of the absolute rights of the latter.[13]

The most efficient means to limit and control power is to counter and oppose it with another power or powers, that is, to pit those with an appetite for ever-increasing power against each other:

> To prevent the abuse of power, it is necessary, that, by the very disposition of things, power should be a check to power.[14]

[Experience has proven] the necessity of permanent laws, to restrain the passions and vices of men, and to secure to the citizens the blessings of society, in the peaceable enjoyment of their lives, liberties, and properties; and the necessity of different orders of men, with various and opposite powers, prerogatives, and privileges, to watch over one another, to balance each other, and to compel each other at all times to be real guardians of the laws.[15]

Experience [has] ever shown, that education as well as religion, aristocracy as well as democracy and monarchy, are, singly, totally inadequate to the business of restraining the passions of men, of preserving a steady government, and protecting the lives, liberties, and properties of the people. Nothing has ever effected it but three different orders of men, bound by their interests to watch over each other, and stand the guardians of the laws. Religion, superstition, oaths, education, laws, all give way before passions, interest, and power, which can be resisted only by passions, interest and power.[16]

Orders of men, watching and balancing each other are the only security; power must be opposed to power, and interest to interest.[17]

For just as the people and their property are protected by the laws, the laws themselves are protected by the structure of government, by arranging the powers of society in such a way as to ensure that no one man or body of men gets hold of all power at once.

First and foremost is the power to make law. Laws must be made, and so that power can check power, they must be made by more than one person; thus the lawmaking power is vested in a legislature, in an assembly of lawmakers.

But within the legislature, power must also check power; therefore, the lawmaking power should be divided into three parts — the one, the few, and the many: a single executive and two lawmaking assemblies, a senate, and a house of representatives, with each power checking the powers of the others, creating a balance.

And once laws have been made, once they have been written and enacted, once they have been legislated, they must be executed and adjudicated. And so that power can check power, the legislative, executive, and judicial powers must be divided and separated, placing each of the three powers into different hands.

This "complication of machinery, all these wheels within wheels," these continually rotating circles of power, preserve and protect the law, and thus the society, the body politic, the people and their property;[18] all hands having a piece of power but none having all, so that the laws alone prevail:

> It is only in a mixed government, of three independent orders, of the one, the few, and the many, and three separate powers, the legislative, executive, and judicial, that all sorts of factions, those of the poor and the rich, those of the gentlemen and common people, those of the one, the few, and the many, can at all times be quelled.[19]

The legislature is so divided into three branches, that no law can be passed in a passion, nor inconsistent with the constitution. The executive is excluded from the two legislative assemblies; and the judiciary power is independent, as well as separate from all.[20]

This is the only scientific government; the only plan which takes into consideration all the principles in nature.[21]

And while the governmental institutions check and balance each other, the people themselves retain the power to check the government, through frequent elections, by removing and replacing, either directly or indirectly, those that enact, execute, and adjudicate the laws. For in doing so, the people ensure that all legislation, execution, and adjudication operate with the consent of the people, the consent of the governed:

All power residing originally in the people, and being derived from them, the several magistrates and officers of government, vested with authority, whether legislative, executive, or judicial, are their substitutes and agents, and are at all times accountable to them.[22]

Therefore, the people alone have an incontestable, unalienable, and indefeasible right to institute government; and to reform, alter, or totally change the same, when their protection, safety, prosperity, and happiness require it.[22]

Thus is created, a republic, a free and democratic, mixed and balanced republic: a government of laws to which all are subject; where the laws are enacted, executed, and adjudicated by those chosen by the people; where the law-making power is divided and balanced and where the laws are legislated, executed, and adjudicated by different hands, in different departments, all watching each other, protecting and defending their own powers while checking the powers of the others.

This republican system of government permeates American society from top to bottom. In the United States, at all levels of government, the people choose their own rulers, either directly or indirectly. At all levels of government, the people are governed by laws and not by men, laws made by more than one person, by numerous and varied assemblies of lawmakers. And at all levels of government, the laws are legislated, executed, and adjudicated by different hands.

For the United States is a republic of republics; each state, county, city, and town, along with the nation itself, is an individual body politic with a republican form of government.

For republican government has proven to be the best of governments, the only form of government wherein the people retain the authority to freely govern themselves:

> In the greatest improvements of society, government will be in the republican form. It is a fixed principle ... that all good government is and must be republican ... a government in which the people have collectively, of by representation, an essential share in the sovereignty.[23]

Representations, instead of collections, of the people; a total separation of the executive from the legislative power, and of the judicial from both; and a balance in the legislature, by three independent, equal branches, are perhaps the only three discoveries in the constitution of a free government, since the institution of Lycurgus [in ancient Greece].[24]

As the [purpose] of government is the greatest happiness of the greatest number, saving at the same time the stipulated rights of all, governments like these, where a large share of power is preserved by the people, deserve to be admired and imitated. It is in such governments that human nature appears in its dignity, honest, brave and generous.[25]

All other forms of government have been tried, retried, and tried again. But in republican governments alone, have the people been secure in their liberty and property for any extended period of time.

And the liberties of the people, the public liberty, must be maintained:

> The sacred rights of mankind are not to be rummaged for, among old parchments, or musty records. They are written, as with a sunbeam, in the whole volume of human nature, by the hand of the divinity itself; and can never be erased or obscured by mortal power.[26]

> A Constitution of government once changed from freedom can never be restored. Liberty once lost is lost forever. When the people once surrender their share

in the legislature, and their right of defending the limitations upon the government, and of resisting every encroachment upon them, they can never regain it.[27]

Be it remembered ... that liberty must at all hazards be supported. We have a right to it, derived from our maker. But if we had not, our fathers have earned and bought it for us, at the expense of their ease, their estates, their pleasure and their blood. And liberty cannot be preserved without a general knowledge among the people, who have a right, from the frame of their nature, to knowledge, as their great Creator, who does nothing in vain, has given them understandings, and a desire to know; but besides this, they have a right, an indisputable, unalienable, indefeasible, divine right to that most dreaded and envied kind of knowledge, I mean, of the characters and conduct of their rulers. Rulers are no more than attorneys, agents, and trustees, for the people; and if the cause, the interest and trust, is insidiously betrayed, or wantonly trifled away, the people have a right to revoke the authority that they themselves have deputed, and to constitute abler and better agents, attorneys, and trustees.[28]

The fact is certain; and wherever a general knowledge and sensibility have prevailed among the people, arbitrary government and every kind of oppression have lessened and disappeared in proportion ... the love of power, which has been so often the cause of slavery, has, whenever freedom has existed, been the cause of freedom. If it is this principle that has always prompted the princes and nobles of the earth, by every species of fraud and violence to shake off all the limitations of their power, it is the same that has always stimulated the common people to aspire at independency, and to endeavor at confining the power of the great within the limits of equity and reason.[29]

In republican governments, the people retain the power to maintain their own liberties and, when necessary, rein in their own rulers. But since republican governments have risen and fallen as other forms of government have, only in well-ordered, constitutional, republican governments, with powers limited and controlled, can the liberties of the people, the public liberty, be properly protected and preserved:

> The best republics will be virtuous, and have been so; but we may hazard a conjecture, that the virtues have been the effect of the well-ordered constitution, rather than the cause.[30]

> All that men can do, is to modify, organize, and arrange the powers of human society, that is to say, the physical strength and force of men, in the best manner to protect, secure, and cherish ... all the natural rights of mankind.[31]

> The political liberty of the citizen is a tranquility of mind, arising from the opinion each person has of his safety. In order to have this liberty, it is requisite the government be so constituted, as that one citizen need not be afraid of another citizen.[32]

> The way to secure liberty is to place it in the people's hands, that is, to give them the power at all times to defend it in the legislature and in the courts of justice.[33]

In the course of world history, the occurrence of free peoples governing themselves has been extremely rare. And, more often than not, self-government wherever it did occur, was short-lived; for free peoples, due in large part to the deficiencies of their governments, quickly descended into tyranny and anarchy.

The American founders, however, knew from their study of history that government, if carefully designed and constructed, could both preserve a free people and serve as a bulwark against the forces of tyranny and anarchy.

Therefore, having been granted the opportunity to create a government for themselves and their posterity, the American founders, using the wisdom of the ages, bequeathed to their posterity a government that after they were gone, would stand the test of time. They bequeathed to their posterity, a government of ordered liberty, a republican government: a free and democratic, mixed and balanced republic.

> — Thirteen governments thus founded on the natural authority of the people alone, without a pretence of miracle or mystery, which are destined to spread over the northern part of that whole quarter of the globe, are a great point gained in favor of the rights of mankind. The experiment is made, and has completely succeeded.[34]

APPENDIX I

Thoughts on Government
— John Adams

In the spring of 1776, as the American colonies were moving inexorably toward independence, the individual colonies began to contemplate what would replace their existing royal governments: what form they would take, how they would function, etc. For assistance they turned to John Adams, who possessed "more learning probably, both ancient and modern, than any man who subscribed the Declaration of Independence." [1]

Adams subsequently wrote "Thoughts on Government," which laid out his recommendations for plans of government for the people of the United States, the ideas of which produced the constitution of Massachusetts (which Adams himself wrote) and those of the other colonies. And the principles contained in these individual constitutions directly influenced the drafting of a constitution for the whole nation: the Constitution of the United States of America.

Never before had so many people been granted the opportunity to actually plan their own governance. And the most remarkable and prolific period of constitution-making in the history of the world can be traced to this short work.

MY DEAR SIR, — If I was equal to the task of forming a plan for the government of a colony, I should be flattered with your request, and very happy to comply with it; because, as the divine science of politics is the science of social happiness, and the blessings of society depend entirely on the constitutions of government, which are generally institutions that last for many generations, there can be no employment more agreeable to a benevolent mind than a research after the best.

> Pope flattered tyrants too much when he said,
> "For forms of government let fools contest,
> That which is best administered is best."

Nothing can be more fallacious than this. But poets read history to collect flowers, not fruits; they attend to fanciful images, not the effects of social institutions. Nothing is more certain, from the history of nations and nature of man, than that some forms of government are better fitted for being well administered than others.

We ought to consider what is the end of government, before we determine which is the best form. Upon this point all speculative politicians will agree, that the happiness of society is the end of government, as all divines and moral philosophers will agree that the happiness of the individual is the end of man. From this principle it will follow, that the form of government which communicates ease, comfort, security, or, in one word, happiness, to the greatest number of persons, and in the greatest degree, is the best.

All sober inquirers after truth, ancient and modern, pagan and Christian, have declared that the happiness of man, as well as his dignity, consists in virtue. Confucius, Zoroaster, Socrates, Mahomet, not to mention authorities really sacred, have agreed in this.

If there is a form of government, then, whose principle and foundation is virtue, will not every sober man acknowledge it better calculated to promote the general happiness than any other form?

Fear is the foundation of most governments; but it is so sordid and brutal a passion, and renders men in whose breasts it predominates so stupid and miserable, that Americans will not be likely to approve of any political institution which is founded on it.

Honor is truly sacred, but holds a lower rank in the scale of moral excellence than virtue. Indeed, the former is but a part of the latter, and consequently has not equal pretensions to support a frame of government productive of human happiness.

The foundation of every government is some principle or passion in the minds of the people. The noblest principles and most generous affections in our nature, then, have the fairest chance to support the noblest and most generous models of government.

A man must be indifferent to the sneers of modern English men, to mention in their company the names of Sidney, Harrington, Locke, Milton, Nedham, Neville, Burnet, and Hoadly. No small fortitude is necessary to confess that one has read them. The wretched condition of this country, however, for ten or fifteen years past, has frequently reminded me of their principles and reasonings. They will convince any candid mind, that there is no good government but what is republican. That the only valuable part of the British constitution is so; because the very definition of a republic is "an empire of laws, and not of men." That, as a republic is the best of governments, so that particular arrangement of the powers of society, or, in other words, that form of government which is best contrived to secure an impartial and exact execution of the laws, is the best of republics.

Of republics there is an inexhaustible variety, because the possible combinations of the powers of society are capable of innumerable variations.

As good government is an empire of laws, how shall your laws be made? In a large society, inhabiting an extensive country, it is impossible that the whole should assemble to make laws. The first necessary step, then, is to depute power from the many to a few of the most wise and good. But by what rules shall you choose your representatives? Agree upon the number and qualifications of persons who shall have the benefit of choosing, or annex this privilege to the inhabitants of a certain extent of ground.

The principal difficulty lies, and the greatest care should be employed, in constituting this representative assembly. It should be in miniature an exact portrait of the people at large. It should think, feel, reason, and act like them. That it may be the interest of this assembly to do strict justice at all times, it should be an equal representation, or, in other words, equal interests among the people should have equal interests in it. Great care should be taken to effect this, and to prevent unfair, partial, and corrupt elections. Such regulations, however, may be better made in times of greater tranquility than the present; and they will spring up themselves naturally, when all the powers of government come to be in the hands of the people's friends. At present, it will be safest to proceed in all established modes, to which the people have been familiarized by habit.

A representation of the people in one assembly being obtained, a question arises, whether all the powers of government, legislative, executive, and judicial, shall be left in this body? I think a people cannot be long free, nor ever happy, whose government is in one assembly. My reasons for this opinion are as follow:--

1. A single assembly is liable to all the vices, follies, and frailties of an individual; subject to fits of humor, starts of passion, flights of enthusiasm, partialities, or prejudice, and consequently productive of hasty results and absurd judgments. And all these errors ought to be corrected and defects supplied by some controlling power.

2. A single assembly is apt to be avaricious, and in time will not scruple to exempt itself from burdens, which it will lay, without compunction, on its constituents.

3. A single assembly is apt to grow ambitious, and after a time will not hesitate to vote itself perpetual. This was one fault of the Long Parliament; but more remarkably of Holland, whose assembly first voted themselves from annual to septennial, then for life, and after a course of years, that all vacancies happening by death or otherwise, should be filled by themselves, without any application to constituents at all.

4. A representative assembly, although extremely well qualified, and absolutely necessary, as a branch of the legislative, is unfit to exercise the executive power, for want of two essential properties, secrecy and dispatch.

5. A representative assembly is still less qualified for the judicial power, because it is too numerous, too slow, and too little skilled in the laws.

6. Because a single assembly, possessed of all the powers of government, would make arbitrary laws for their own interest, execute all laws arbitrarily for their own interest, and adjudge all controversies in their own favor.

But shall the whole power of legislation rest in one assembly? Most of the foregoing reasons apply equally to prove that the legislative power ought to be more complex; to which we may add, that if the legislative power is wholly in one assembly, and the executive in another, or in a single person, these two powers will oppose and encroach upon each other, until the contest shall end in war, and the whole power, legislative and executive, be usurped by the strongest.

The judicial power, in such case, could not mediate, or hold the balance between the two contending powers, because the legislative would undermine it. And this shows the necessity; too, of giving the executive power a negative upon the legislative, otherwise this will be continually encroaching upon that.

To avoid these dangers, let a distinct assembly be constituted, as a mediator between the two extreme branches of the legislature, that which represents the people, and that which is vested with the executive power.

Let the representative assembly then elect by ballot, from among themselves or their constituents, or both, a distinct assembly, which, for the sake of perspicuity, we will call a council. It may consist of any number you please, say twenty or thirty, and should have a free and independent exercise of its judgment, and consequently a negative voice in the legislature.

These two bodies, thus constituted, and made integral parts of the legislature, let them unite, and by joint ballot choose a governor, who, after being stripped of most of those badges of domination, called prerogatives, should have a free and independent exercise of his judgment, and be made also an integral part of the legislature. This, I know, is liable to objections; and, if you please, you may make him only president of the council, as in Connecticut. But as the governor is to be invested with the executive power, with consent of council, I think he ought to have a negative upon the legislative. If he is annually elective, as he ought to be, he will always have so much reverence and affection for the people, their representatives and counselors, that, although you give him an independent exercise of his judgment, he will seldom use it in opposition to the two houses, except in cases the public utility of which would be conspicuous; and some such cases would happen.

In the present exigency of American affairs, when, by an act of Parliament, we are put out of the royal protection, and consequently discharged from our allegiance, and it has become necessary to assume government for our immediate security, the governor, lieutenant-governor, secretary, treasurer, commissary, attorney-general, should be chosen by joint ballot of both houses. And these and all other elections, especially of representatives and counselors, should be annual, there not being in the whole circle of the sciences a maxim more infallible than this, "where annual elections end, there slavery begins."

> These great men, in this respect, should be, once a year,
> "Like bubbles on the sea of matter borne,
>   They rise, they break, and to that sea return."

This will teach them the great political virtues of humility, patience, and moderation, without which every man in power becomes a ravenous beast of prey.

This mode of constituting the great offices of state will answer very well for the present; but if by experiment it should be found inconvenient, the legislature may, at its leisure, devise other methods of creating them, by elections of the people at large, as in Connecticut, or it may enlarge the term for which they shall be chosen to seven years, or three years, or for life, or make any other alterations which the society shall find productive of its ease, its safety, its freedom, or, in one word, its happiness.

A rotation of all offices, as well as of representatives and counselors, has many advocates, and is contended for with many plausible arguments. It would be attended, no doubt, with many advantages; and if the society has a sufficient number of suitable characters to supply the great number of vacancies which would be made by such a rotation, I can see no objection to it. These persons may be allowed to serve for three years, and then be excluded three years, or for any longer or shorter term.

Any seven or nine of the legislative council may be made a quorum, for doing business as a privy council, to advise the governor in the exercise of the executive branch of power, and in all acts of state.

The governor should have the command of the militia and of all your armies. The power of pardons should be with the governor and council.

Judges, justices, and all other officers, civil and military, should be nominated and appointed by the governor, with the advice and consent of council, unless you choose to have a government more popular; if you do, all officers, civil and military, may be chosen by joint ballot of both houses; or, in order to preserve the independence and importance of each house, by ballot of one house, concurred in by the other. Sheriffs should be chosen by the freeholders of counties; so should registers of deeds and clerks of counties.

All officers should have commissions, under the hand of the governor and seal of the colony.

The dignity and stability of government in all its branches, the morals of the people, and every blessing of society depend so much upon an upright and skillful administration of justice, that the judicial power ought to be distinct from both the legislative and executive, and independent upon both, that so it may be a check upon both, as both should be checks upon that. The judges, therefore, should be always men of learning and experience in the laws, of exemplary morals, great patience, calmness, coolness, and attention. Their minds should not be distracted with jarring interests; they should not be dependent upon any man, or body of men. To these ends, they should hold estates for life in their offices; or, in other words, their commissions should be during good behavior, and their salaries ascertained and established by law. For misbehavior, the grand inquest of the colony, the house of representatives, should impeach them before the governor and council, where they should have time and opportunity to make their defense; but, if convicted, should be removed from their offices, and subjected to such other punishment as shall be thought proper.

A militia law, requiring all men, or with very few exceptions besides cases of conscience, to be provided with arms and ammunition, to be trained at certain seasons; and requiring counties, towns, or other small districts, to be provided with public stocks of ammunition and entrenching utensils, and with some settled plans for transporting provisions after the militia, when marched to defend their country against sudden invasions; and requiring certain districts to be provided with field-pieces, companies of mattresses, and perhaps some regiments of light-horse, is always a wise institution, and, in the present circumstances of our country, indispensable.

Laws for the liberal education of youth, especially of the lower class of people, are so extremely wise and useful, that, to a humane and generous mind, no expense for this purpose would be thought extravagant.

The very mention of sumptuary laws will excite a smile. Whether our countrymen have wisdom and virtue enough to submit to them, I know not; but the happiness of the people might be greatly promoted by them, and a revenue saved sufficient to carry on this war forever. Frugality is a great revenue, besides curing us of vanities, levities, and fopperies, which are real antidotes to all great, manly, and warlike virtues.

But must not all commissions run in the name of a king? No. Why may they not as well run thus, "The colony of to A. B. greeting," and be tested by the governor?

Why may not writs, instead of running in the name of the king, run thus, "The colony of to the sheriff," &c., and be tested by the chief justice?

Why may not indictments conclude, "against the peace of the colony of and the dignity of the same?"

A constitution founded on these principles introduces knowledge among the people, and inspires them with a conscious dignity becoming freemen; a general emulation takes place, which causes good humor, sociability, good manners, and good morals to be general. That elevation of sentiment inspired by such a government, makes the common people brave and enterprising. That ambition which is inspired by it makes them sober, industrious, and frugal. You will find among them some elegance, perhaps, but more solidity; a little pleasure, but a great deal of business; some politeness, but more civility. If you compare such a country with the regions of domination, whether monarchical or aristocratical, you will fancy yourself in Arcadia or Elysium.

If the colonies should assume governments separately, they should be left entirely to their own choice of the forms; and if a continental constitution should be formed, it should be a congress, containing a fair and adequate representation of the colonies, and its authority should sacredly be confined to these cases, namely, war, trade, disputes between colony and colony, the post office, and the unappropriated lands of the crown, as they used to be called.

These colonies, under such forms of government, and in such a union, would be unconquerable by all the monarchies of Europe.

You and I, my dear friend, have been sent into life at a time when the greatest lawgivers of antiquity would have wished to live. How few of the human race have ever enjoyed an opportunity of making an election of government, more than of air, soil, or climate, for themselves or their children! When, before the present epocha, had three millions of people full power and a fair opportunity to form and establish the wisest and happiest government that human wisdom can contrive? I hope you will avail yourself and your country of that extensive learning and indefatigable industry which you possess, to assist her in the formation of the happiest governments and the best character of a great people. For myself, I must beg you to keep my name out of sight; for this feeble attempt, if it should be known to be mine, would oblige me to apply to myself those lines of the immortal John Milton, in one of his sonnets:--

> "I did but prompt the age to quit their clogs
> By the known rules of ancient liberty,
> When straight a barbarous noise environs me
> Of owls and cuckoos, asses, apes, and dogs."

Appendix II

The Constitution of the United States

We the People of the United States, in Order to form a more perfect Union, establish Justice, insure domestic Tranquility, provide for the common defence, promote the general Welfare, and secure the Blessings of Liberty to ourselves and our Posterity, do ordain and establish this Constitution for the United States of America.

Article. I.

Section. 1. All legislative Powers herein granted shall be vested in a Congress of the United States, which shall consist of a Senate and House of Representatives.

Section. 2. The House of Representatives shall be composed of Members chosen every second Year by the People of the several States, and the Electors in each State shall have the Qualifications requisite for Electors of the most numerous Branch of the State Legislature.

No Person shall be a Representative who shall not have attained to the Age of twenty five Years, and been seven Years a Citizen of the United States, and who shall not, when elected, be an Inhabitant of that State in which he shall be chosen.

Representatives and direct Taxes shall be apportioned among the several States which may be included within this Union, according to their respective Numbers, which shall be determined by adding to the whole Number of free Persons, including those bound to Service for a Term of Years, and excluding Indians not taxed, three fifths of all other Persons. The actual Enumeration shall be made within three Years after the first Meeting of the Congress of the United States, and within every subsequent Term of ten Years, in such Manner as they shall by Law direct. The Number of Representatives shall not exceed one for every thirty Thousand, but each State shall have at Least one Representative; and until such enumeration shall be made, the State of New Hampshire shall be entitled to chuse three, Massachusetts eight, Rhode-Island and Providence Plantations one, Connecticut five, New-York six, New Jersey four, Pennsylvania eight, Delaware one, Maryland six, Virginia ten, North Carolina five, South Carolina five, and Georgia three.

When vacancies happen in the Representation from any State, the Executive Authority thereof shall issue Writs of Election to fill such Vacancies.

The House of Representatives shall chuse their Speaker and other Officers; and shall have the sole Power of Impeachment.

Section. 3. The Senate of the United States shall be composed of two Senators from each State, chosen by the Legislature thereof, for six Years; and each Senator shall have one Vote.

Immediately after they shall be assembled in Consequence of the first Election, they shall be divided as equally as may be into three Classes. The Seats of the Senators of the first Class shall be vacated at the Expiration of the second Year, of the second Class at the Expiration of the fourth Year, and of the third Class at the Expiration of the sixth Year, so that one third may be chosen every second Year; and if Vacancies happen by Resignation, or otherwise, during the Recess of the Legislature of any State, the Executive thereof may make temporary Appointments until the next Meeting of the Legislature, which shall then fill such Vacancies.

No Person shall be a Senator who shall not have attained to the Age of thirty Years, and been nine Years a Citizen of the United States, and who shall not, when elected, be an Inhabitant of that State for which he shall be chosen.

The Vice President of the United States shall be President of the Senate, but shall have no Vote, unless they be equally divided.

The Senate shall chuse their other Officers, and also a President pro tempore, in the Absence of the Vice President, or when he shall exercise the Office of President of the United States.

The Senate shall have the sole Power to try all Impeachments. When sitting for that Purpose, they shall be on Oath or Affirmation. When the President of the United States is tried, the Chief Justice shall preside: And no Person shall be convicted without the Concurrence of two thirds of the Members present.

Judgment in Cases of Impeachment shall not extend further than to removal from Office, and disqualification to hold and enjoy any Office of honor, Trust or Profit under the United States: but the Party convicted shall nevertheless be liable and subject to Indictment, Trial, Judgment and Punishment, according to Law.

Section. 4.The Times, Places and Manner of holding Elections for Senators and Representatives, shall be prescribed in each State by the Legislature thereof; but the Congress may at any time by Law make or alter such Regulations, except as to the Places of chusing Senators.

The Congress shall assemble at least once in every Year, and such Meeting shall be on the first Monday in December, unless they shall by Law appoint a different Day.

Section. 5. Each House shall be the Judge of the Elections, Returns and Qualifications of its own Members, and a Majority of each shall constitute a Quorum to do Business; but a smaller Number may adjourn from day to day, and may be authorized to compel the Attendance of absent Members, in such Manner, and under such Penalties as each House may provide.

Each House may determine the Rules of its Proceedings, punish its Members for disorderly Behaviour, and, with the Concurrence of two thirds, expel a Member.

Each House shall keep a Journal of its Proceedings, and from time to time publish the same, excepting such Parts as may in their Judgment require Secrecy; and the Yeas and Nays of the Members of either House on any question shall, at the Desire of one fifth of those Present, be entered on the Journal.

Neither House, during the Session of Congress, shall, without the Consent of the other, adjourn for more than three days, nor to any other Place than that in which the two Houses shall be sitting.

Section. 6. The Senators and Representatives shall receive a Compensation for their Services, to be ascertained by Law, and paid out of the Treasury of the United States. They shall in all Cases, except Treason, Felony and Breach of the Peace, be privileged from Arrest during their Attendance at the Session of their respective Houses, and in going to and returning from the same; and for any Speech or Debate in either House, they shall not be questioned in any other Place.

No Senator or Representative shall, during the Time for which he was elected, be appointed to any civil Office under the Authority of the United States, which shall have been created, or the Emoluments whereof shall have been encreased during such time; and no Person holding any Office under the United States, shall be a Member of either House during his Continuance in Office.

Section. 7. All Bills for raising Revenue shall originate in the House of Representatives; but the Senate may propose or concur with Amendments as on other Bills.

Every Bill which shall have passed the House of Representatives and the Senate, shall, before it become a Law, be presented to the President of the United States; If he approve he shall sign it, but if not he shall return it, with his Objections to that House in which it shall have originated, who shall enter the Objections at large on their Journal, and proceed to reconsider it. If after such Reconsideration two thirds of that House shall agree to pass the Bill, it shall be sent, together with the Objections, to the other House, by which it shall likewise be reconsidered, and if approved by two thirds of that House, it shall become a Law. But in all such Cases the Votes of both Houses shall be determined by yeas and Nays, and the Names of the Persons voting for and against the Bill shall be entered on the Journal of each House respectively. If any Bill shall not be returned by the President within ten Days (Sundays excepted) after it shall have been presented to him, the Same shall be a Law, in like Manner as if he had signed it, unless the Congress by their Adjournment prevent its Return, in which Case it shall not be a Law.

Every Order, Resolution, or Vote to which the Concurrence of the Senate and House of Representatives may be necessary (except on a question of Adjournment) shall be presented to the President of the United States; and before the Same shall take Effect, shall be approved by him, or being disapproved by him, shall be repassed by two thirds of the Senate and House of Representatives, according to the Rules and Limitations prescribed in the Case of a Bill.

Section. 8. The Congress shall have Power To lay and collect Taxes, Duties, Imposts and Excises, to pay the Debts and provide for the common Defence and general Welfare of the United States; but all Duties, Imposts and Excises shall be uniform throughout the United States;

To borrow Money on the credit of the United States;

To regulate Commerce with foreign Nations, and among the several States, and with the Indian Tribes;

To establish an uniform Rule of Naturalization, and uniform Laws on the subject of Bankruptcies throughout the United States;

To coin Money, regulate the Value thereof, and of foreign Coin, and fix the Standard of Weights and Measures;

To provide for the Punishment of counterfeiting the Securities and current Coin of the United States;

To establish Post Offices and post Roads;

To promote the Progress of Science and useful Arts, by securing for limited Times to Authors and Inventors the exclusive Right to their respective Writings and Discoveries;

To constitute Tribunals inferior to the supreme Court;

To define and punish Piracies and Felonies committed on the high Seas, and Offences against the Law of Nations;

To declare War, grant Letters of Marque and Reprisal, and make Rules concerning Captures on Land and Water;

To raise and support Armies, but no Appropriation of Money to that Use shall be for a longer Term than two Years;

To provide and maintain a Navy;

To make Rules for the Government and Regulation of the land and naval Forces;

To provide for calling forth the Militia to execute the Laws of the Union, suppress Insurrections and repel Invasions;

To provide for organizing, arming, and disciplining, the Militia, and for governing such Part of them as may be employed in the Service of the United States, reserving to the States respectively, the Appointment of the Officers, and the Authority of training the Militia according to the discipline prescribed by Congress;

To exercise exclusive Legislation in all Cases whatsoever, over such District (not exceeding ten Miles square) as may, by Cession of particular States, and the Acceptance of Congress, become the Seat of the Government of the United States, and to exercise like Authority over all Places purchased by the Consent of the Legislature of the State in which the Same shall be, for the Erection of Forts, Magazines, Arsenals, dock-Yards, and other needful Buildings; — And

To make all Laws which shall be necessary and proper for carrying into Execution the foregoing Powers, and all other Powers vested by this Constitution in the Government of the United States, or in any Department or Officer thereof.

Section. 9. The Migration or Importation of such Persons as any of the States now existing shall think proper to admit, shall not be prohibited by the Congress prior to the Year one thousand eight hundred and eight, but a Tax or duty may be imposed on such Importation, not exceeding ten dollars for each Person.

The Privilege of the Writ of Habeas Corpus shall not be suspended, unless when in Cases of Rebellion or Invasion the public Safety may require it.

No Bill of Attainder or ex post facto Law shall be passed.

No Capitation, or other direct, Tax shall be laid, unless in Proportion to the Census or Enumeration herein before directed to be taken.

No Tax or Duty shall be laid on Articles exported from any State.

No Preference shall be given by any Regulation of Commerce or Revenue to the Ports of one State over those of another; nor shall Vessels bound to, or from, one State, be obliged to enter, clear, or pay Duties in another.

No Money shall be drawn from the Treasury, but in Consequence of Appropriations made by Law; and a regular Statement and Account of the Receipts and Expenditures of all public Money shall be published from time to time.

No Title of Nobility shall be granted by the United States: And no Person holding any Office of Profit or Trust under them, shall, without the Consent of the Congress, accept of any present, Emolument, Office, or Title, of any kind whatever, from any King, Prince, or foreign State.

Section. 10. No State shall enter into any Treaty, Alliance, or Confederation; grant Letters of Marque and Reprisal; coin Money; emit Bills of Credit; make any Thing but gold and silver Coin a Tender in Payment of Debts; pass any Bill of Attainder, ex post facto Law, or Law impairing the Obligation of Contracts, or grant any Title of Nobility.

No State shall, without the Consent of the Congress, lay any Imposts or Duties on Imports or Exports, except what may be absolutely necessary for executing it's inspection Laws; and the net Produce of all Duties and Imposts, laid by any State on Imports or Exports, shall be for the Use of the Treasury of the United States; and all such Laws shall be subject to the Revision and Controul of the Congress.

No State shall, without the Consent of Congress, lay any Duty of Tonnage, keep Troops, or Ships of War in time of Peace, enter into any Agreement or Compact with another State, or with a foreign Power, or engage in War, unless actually invaded, or in such imminent Danger as will not admit of delay.

Article. II.

Section. 1. The executive Power shall be vested in a President of the United States of America. He shall hold his Office during the Term of four Years, and, together with the Vice President, chosen for the same Term, be elected, as follows:

Each State shall appoint, in such Manner as the Legislature thereof may direct, a Number of Electors, equal to the whole Number of Senators and Representatives to which the State may be entitled in the Congress: but no Senator or Representative, or Person holding an Office of Trust or Profit under the United States, shall be appointed an Elector.

The Electors shall meet in their respective States, and vote by Ballot for two Persons, of whom one at least shall not be an Inhabitant of the same State with themselves. And they shall make a List of all the Persons voted for, and of the Number of Votes for each; which List they shall sign and certify, and transmit sealed to the Seat of the Government of the United States, directed to the President of the Senate. The President of the Senate shall, in the Presence of the Senate and House of Representatives, open all the Certificates, and the Votes shall then be counted. The Person having the greatest Number of Votes shall be the President, if such Number be a Majority of the whole Number of Electors appointed; and if there be more than one who have such Majority, and have an equal Number of Votes, then the House of Representatives shall immediately chuse by Ballot one of them for President; and if no Person have a Majority, then from the five highest on the List the said House shall in like Manner chuse the President. But in chusing the President, the Votes shall be taken by States, the Representation from each State having one Vote; a quorum for this Purpose shall consist of a Member or Members from two thirds of the States, and a Majority of all the States shall be necessary to a Choice. In every Case, after the Choice of the President, the Person having the greatest Number of Votes of the Electors shall be the Vice President. But if there should remain two or more who have equal Votes, the Senate shall chuse from them by Ballot the Vice President.

The Congress may determine the Time of chusing the Electors, and the Day on which they shall give their Votes; which Day shall be the same throughout the United States.

No Person except a natural born Citizen, or a Citizen of the United States, at the time of the Adoption of this Constitution, shall be eligible to the Office of President; neither shall any Person be eligible to that Office who shall not have attained to the Age of thirty five Years, and been fourteen Years a Resident within the United States.

In Case of the Removal of the President from Office, or of his Death, Resignation, or Inability to discharge the Powers and Duties of the said Office, the Same shall devolve on the Vice President, and the Congress may by Law provide for the Case of Removal, Death, Resignation or Inability, both of the President and Vice President, declaring what Officer shall then act as President, and such Officer shall act accordingly, until the Disability be removed, or a President shall be elected.

The President shall, at stated Times, receive for his Services, a Compensation, which shall neither be increased nor diminished during the Period for which he shall have been elected, and he shall not receive within that Period any other Emolument from the United States, or any of them.

Before he enter on the Execution of his Office, he shall take the following Oath or Affirmation: — "I do solemnly swear (or affirm) that I will faithfully execute the Office of President of the United States, and will to the best of my Ability, preserve, protect and defend the Constitution of the United States."

Section. 2. The President shall be Commander in Chief of the Army and Navy of the United States, and of the Militia of the several States, when called into the actual Service of the United States; he may require the Opinion, in writing, of the principal Officer in each of the executive Departments, upon any Subject relating to the Duties of their respective Offices, and he shall have Power to grant Reprieves and Pardons for Offences against the United States, except in Cases of Impeachment.

He shall have Power, by and with the Advice and Consent of the Senate, to make Treaties, provided two thirds of the Senators present concur; and he shall nominate, and by and with the Advice and Consent of the Senate, shall appoint Ambassadors, other public Ministers and Consuls, Judges of the supreme Court, and all other Officers of the United States, whose Appointments are not herein otherwise provided for, and which shall be established by Law: but the Congress may by Law vest the Appointment of such inferior Officers, as they think proper, in the President alone, in the Courts of Law, or in the Heads of Departments.

The President shall have Power to fill up all Vacancies that may happen during the Recess of the Senate, by granting Commissions which shall expire at the End of their next Session.

Section. 3. He shall from time to time give to the Congress Information of the State of the Union, and recommend to their Consideration such Measures as he shall judge necessary and expedient; he may, on extraordinary Occasions, convene both Houses, or either of them, and in Case of Disagreement between them, with Respect to the Time of Adjournment, he may adjourn them to such Time as he shall think proper; he shall receive Ambassadors and other public Ministers; he shall take Care that the Laws be faithfully executed, and shall Commission all the Officers of the United States.

Section. 4. The President, Vice President and all civil Officers of the United States, shall be removed from Office on Impeachment for, and Conviction of, Treason, Bribery, or other high Crimes and Misdemeanors.

Article. III.

Section. 1. The judicial Power of the United States shall be vested in one supreme Court, and in such inferior Courts as the Congress may from time to time ordain and establish. The Judges, both of the supreme and inferior Courts, shall hold their Offices during good Behaviour, and shall, at stated Times, receive for their Services a Compensation, which shall not be diminished during their Continuance in Office.

Section. 2. The judicial Power shall extend to all Cases, in Law and Equity, arising under this Constitution, the Laws of the

United States, and Treaties made, or which shall be made, under their Authority; — to all Cases affecting Ambassadors, other public Ministers and Consuls; — to all Cases of admiralty and maritime Jurisdiction; — to Controversies to which the United States shall be a Party; — to Controversies between two or more States; — between a State and Citizens of another State; — between Citizens of different States; — between Citizens of the same State claiming Lands under Grants of different States, and between a State, or the Citizens thereof, and foreign States, Citizens or Subjects.

In all Cases affecting Ambassadors, other public Ministers and Consuls, and those in which a State shall be Party, the supreme Court shall have original Jurisdiction. In all the other Cases before mentioned, the supreme Court shall have appellate Jurisdiction, both as to Law and Fact, with such Exceptions, and under such Regulations as the Congress shall make.

The Trial of all Crimes, except in Cases of Impeachment, shall be by Jury; and such Trial shall be held in the State where the said Crimes shall have been committed; but when not committed within any State, the Trial shall be at such Place or Places as the Congress may by Law have directed.

Section. 3. Treason against the United States shall consist only in levying War against them, or in adhering to their Enemies, giving them Aid and Comfort. No Person shall be convicted of Treason unless on the Testimony of two Witnesses to the same overt Act, or on Confession in open Court.

The Congress shall have Power to declare the Punishment of Treason, but no Attainder of Treason shall work Corruption of Blood, or Forfeiture except during the Life of the Person attainted.

Article. IV.

Section. 1. Full Faith and Credit shall be given in each State to the public Acts, Records, and judicial Proceedings of every other State. And the Congress may by general Laws prescribe the Manner in which such Acts, Records and Proceedings shall be proved, and the Effect thereof.

Section. 2. The Citizens of each State shall be entitled to all Privileges and Immunities of Citizens in the several States.

A Person charged in any State with Treason, Felony, or other Crime, who shall flee from Justice, and be found in another State, shall on Demand of the executive Authority of the State from which he fled, be delivered up, to be removed to the State having Jurisdiction of the Crime.

No Person held to Service or Labour in one State, under the Laws thereof, escaping into another, shall, in Consequence of any Law or Regulation therein, be discharged from such Service or Labour, but shall be delivered up on Claim of the Party to whom such Service or Labour may be due.

Section. 3. New States may be admitted by the Congress into this Union; but no new State shall be formed or erected within the Jurisdiction of any other State; nor any State be formed by the Junction of two or more States, or Parts of States, without the Consent of the Legislatures of the States concerned as well as of the Congress.

The Congress shall have Power to dispose of and make all needful Rules and Regulations respecting the Territory or other Property belonging to the United States; and nothing in this Constitution shall be so construed as to Prejudice any Claims of the United States, or of any particular State.

Section. 4. The United States shall guarantee to every State in this Union a Republican Form of Government, and shall protect each of them against Invasion; and on Application of the Legislature, or of the Executive (when the Legislature cannot be convened), against domestic Violence.

Article. V.

The Congress, whenever two thirds of both Houses shall deem it necessary, shall propose Amendments to this Constitution, or, on the Application of the Legislatures of two thirds of the several States, shall call a Convention for proposing Amendments, which, in either Case, shall be valid to all Intents and Purposes, as Part of this Constitution, when ratified by the Legislatures of three fourths of the several States, or by Conventions in three fourths thereof, as the one or the other Mode of Ratification may be proposed by the Congress; Provided that no Amendment which may be made prior to the Year One thousand eight hundred and eight shall in any Manner affect the first and fourth Clauses in the Ninth Section of the first Article; and that no State, without its Consent, shall be deprived of its equal Suffrage in the Senate.

Article. VI.

All Debts contracted and Engagements entered into, before the Adoption of this Constitution, shall be as valid against the United States under this Constitution, as under the Confederation.

This Constitution, and the Laws of the United States which shall be made in Pursuance thereof; and all Treaties made, or which shall be made, under the Authority of the United States, shall be the supreme Law of the Land; and the Judges in every

State shall be bound thereby, any Thing in the Constitution or Laws of any State to the Contrary notwithstanding.

The Senators and Representatives before mentioned, and the Members of the several State Legislatures, and all executive and judicial Officers, both of the United States and of the several States, shall be bound by Oath or Affirmation, to support this Constitution; but no religious Test shall ever be required as a Qualification to any Office or public Trust under the United States.

Article. VII.

The Ratification of the Conventions of nine States, shall be sufficient for the Establishment of this Constitution between the States so ratifying the Same.

done in Convention by the Unanimous Consent of the States present the Seventeenth Day of September in the Year of our Lord one thousand seven hundred and Eighty seven and of the Independence of the United States of America the Twelfth In witness whereof We have hereunto subscribed our Names,

Amendment I

Congress shall make no law respecting an establishment of religion, or prohibiting the free exercise thereof; or abridging the freedom of speech, or of the press; or the right of the people peaceably to assemble, and to petition the Government for a redress of grievances.

Amendment II

A well regulated Militia, being necessary to the security of a free State, the right of the people to keep and bear Arms, shall not be infringed.

Amendment III

No Soldier shall, in time of peace be quartered in any house, without the consent of the Owner, nor in time of war, but in a manner to be prescribed by law.

Amendment IV

The right of the people to be secure in their persons, houses, papers, and effects, against unreasonable searches and seizures, shall not be violated, and no Warrants shall issue, but upon probable cause, supported by Oath or affirmation, and particularly describing the place to be searched, and the persons or things to be seized.

Amendment V

No person shall be held to answer for a capital, or otherwise infamous crime, unless on a presentment or indictment of a Grand Jury, except in cases arising in the land or naval forces, or in the Militia, when in actual service in time of War or public danger; nor shall any person be subject for the same offence to be twice put in jeopardy of life or limb; nor shall be compelled in any criminal case to be a witness against himself, nor be deprived of life, liberty, or property, without due process of law; nor shall private property be taken for public use, without just compensation.

Amendment VI

In all criminal prosecutions, the accused shall enjoy the right to a speedy and public trial, by an impartial jury of the State and district wherein the crime shall have been committed, which district shall have been previously ascertained by law, and to be informed of the nature and cause of the accusation; to be confronted with the witnesses against him; to have compulsory process for obtaining witnesses in his favor, and to have the Assistance of Counsel for his defence.

Amendment VII

In Suits at common law, where the value in controversy shall exceed twenty dollars, the right of trial by jury shall be preserved, and no fact tried by a jury, shall be otherwise re-examined in any Court of the United States, than according to the rules of the common law.

Amendment VIII

Excessive bail shall not be required, nor excessive fines imposed, nor cruel and unusual punishments inflicted.

Amendment XIV

The enumeration in the Constitution, of certain rights, shall not be construed to deny or disparage others retained by the people.

Amendment X

The powers not delegated to the United States by the Constitution, nor prohibited by it to the States, are reserved to the States respectively, or to the people.

Amendment XI

The Judicial power of the United States shall not be construed to extend to any suit in law or equity, commenced or prosecuted against one of the United States by Citizens of another State, or by Citizens or Subjects of any Foreign State.

Amendment XII

The Electors shall meet in their respective states, and vote by ballot for President and Vice-President, one of whom, at least, shall not be an inhabitant of the same state with themselves; they shall name in their ballots the person voted for as President, and in distinct ballots the person voted for as Vice-President, and they shall make distinct lists of all persons voted for as President, and of all persons voted for as Vice-President, and of the number of votes for each, which lists they shall sign and certify, and transmit sealed to the seat of the government of the United States, directed to the President of the Senate; — The President of the Senate shall, in the presence of the Senate and House of Representatives, open all the certificates and the votes shall then be counted; — The person having the greatest number of votes for President, shall be the President, if such number be a majority of the whole number of Electors appointed; and if no person have such majority, then from the persons having the highest numbers not exceeding three on the list of those voted for as President, the House of Representatives shall choose immediately, by ballot, the President. But in choosing the President, the votes shall be taken by states, the representation from each state having one vote; a quorum for this purpose shall consist of a member or members from two-thirds of the states, and a majority of all the states shall be necessary to a choice. And if the House of Representatives shall not choose a President whenever the right of choice shall devolve upon them, before the fourth day of March next following, then the Vice-President shall act as President, as in the case of the death or other constitutional disability of the President. — The person having the greatest number of votes as Vice-President, shall be the Vice-President, if such number be a majority of the whole number of Electors appointed, and if no person have a majority, then from the two highest numbers on the list, the Senate shall choose the Vice-President; a quorum for the purpose shall consist of two-thirds of the whole number of Senators, and a majority of the whole number shall be necessary to a choice. But no person constitutionally ineligible to the office of President shall be eligible to that of Vice-President of the United States.

Amendment XIII

Section. 1. Neither slavery nor involuntary servitude, except as a punishment for crime whereof the party shall have been duly convicted, shall exist within the United States, or any place subject to their jurisdiction.

Section. 2. Congress shall have power to enforce this article by appropriate legislation.

Amendment XIV

Section. 1. All persons born or naturalized in the United States, and subject to the jurisdiction thereof, are citizens of the United States and of the State wherein they reside. No State shall make or enforce any law which shall abridge the privileges or immunities of citizens of the United States; nor shall any State deprive any person of life, liberty, or property, without due process of law; nor deny to any person within its jurisdiction the equal protection of the laws.

Section. 2. Representatives shall be apportioned among the several States according to their respective numbers, counting the whole number of persons in each State, excluding Indians not taxed. But when the right to vote at any election for the choice of electors for President and Vice President of the United States, Representatives in Congress, the Executive and Judicial officers of a State, or the members of the Legislature thereof, is denied to any of the male inhabitants of such State, being twenty-one years of age, and citizens of the United States, or in any way abridged, except for participation in rebellion, or other crime, the basis of representation therein shall be reduced in the proportion which the number of such male citizens shall bear to the whole number of male citizens twenty-one years of age in such State.

Section. 3. No person shall be a Senator or Representative in Congress, or elector of President and Vice President, or hold any office, civil or military, under the United States, or under any State, who, having previously taken an oath, as a member of Congress, or as an officer of the United States, or as a member of any State legislature, or as an executive or judicial officer of any State, to support the Constitution of the United States, shall have engaged in insurrection or rebellion against the same, or given aid or comfort to the enemies thereof. But Congress may by a vote of two-thirds of each House, remove such disability.

Section. 4. The validity of the public debt of the United States, authorized by law, including debts incurred for payment of pensions and bounties for services in suppressing insurrection or rebellion, shall not be questioned. But neither the United States nor any State shall assume or pay any debt or obligation incurred in aid of insurrection or rebellion against the United States, or any claim for the loss or emancipation of any slave; but all such debts, obligations and claims shall be held illegal and void.

Section. 5. The Congress shall have power to enforce, by appropriate legislation, the provisions of this article.

Amendment XV

Section. 1. The right of citizens of the United States to vote shall not be denied or abridged by the United States or by any State on account of race, color, or previous condition of servitude.

Section. 2. The Congress shall have power to enforce this article by appropriate legislation.

Amendment XVI

The Congress shall have power to lay and collect taxes on incomes, from whatever source derived, without apportionment among the several States, and without regard to any census or enumeration.

Amendment XVII

The Senate of the United States shall be composed of two Senators from each State, elected by the people thereof, for six years; and each Senator shall have one vote. The electors in each

State shall have the qualifications requisite for electors of the most numerous branch of the State legislatures.

When vacancies happen in the representation of any State in the Senate, the executive authority of such State shall issue writs of election to fill such vacancies: Provided, That the legislature of any State may empower the executive thereof to make temporary appointments until the people fill the vacancies by election as the legislature may direct.

This amendment shall not be so construed as to affect the election or term of any Senator chosen before it becomes valid as part of the Constitution.

Amendment XVIII

Section. 1. After one year from the ratification of this article the manufacture, sale, or transportation of intoxicating liquors within, the importation thereof into, or the exportation thereof from the United States and all territory subject to the jurisdiction thereof for beverage purposes is hereby prohibited.

Section. 2. The Congress and the several States shall have concurrent power to enforce this article by appropriate legislation.

Section. 3. This article shall be inoperative unless it shall have been ratified as an amendment to the Constitution by the legislatures of the several States, as provided in the Constitution, within seven years from the date of the submission hereof to the States by the Congress.

Amendment XIX

The right of citizens of the United States to vote shall not be denied or abridged by the United States or by any State on account of sex.

Congress shall have power to enforce this article by appropriate legislation.

Amendment XX

Section. 1. The terms of the President and Vice President shall end at noon on the 20th day of January, and the terms of Senators and Representatives at noon on the 3d day of January, of the years in which such terms would have ended if this article had not been ratified; and the terms of their successors shall then begin.

Section. 2. The Congress shall assemble at least once in every year, and such meeting shall begin at noon on the 3d day of January, unless they shall by law appoint a different day.

Section. 3. If, at the time fixed for the beginning of the term of the President, the President elect shall have died, the Vice President elect shall become President. If a President shall not have been chosen before the time fixed for the beginning of his term, or if the President elect shall have failed to qualify, then the Vice President elect shall act as President until a President shall have qualified; and the Congress may by law provide for the case wherein neither a President elect nor a Vice President elect shall have qualified, declaring who shall then act as President, or the manner in which one who is to act shall be selected, and such person shall act accordingly until a President or Vice President shall have qualified.

Section. 4. The Congress may by law provide for the case of the death of any of the persons from whom the House of Representatives may choose a President whenever the right of choice shall have devolved upon them, and for the case of the death of any of the persons from whom the Senate may choose a Vice President whenever the right of choice shall have devolved upon them.

Section. 5. Sections 1 and 2 shall take effect on the 15th day of October following the ratification of this article.

Section. 6. This article shall be inoperative unless it shall have been ratified as an amendment to the Constitution by the legislatures of three-fourths of the several States within seven years from the date of its submission.

Amendment XXI

Section. 1. The eighteenth article of amendment to the Constitution of the United States is hereby repealed.

Section. 2. The transportation or importation into any State, Territory, or possession of the United States for delivery or use therein of intoxicating liquors, in violation of the laws thereof, is hereby prohibited.

Section. 3. This article shall be inoperative unless it shall have been ratified as an amendment to the Constitution by conventions in the several States, as provided in the Constitution, within seven years from the date of the submission hereof to the States by the Congress.

Amendment XXII

Section. 1. No person shall be elected to the office of the President more than twice, and no person who has held the office of President, or acted as President, for more than two years of a term to which some other person was elected President shall be elected to the office of the President more than once. But this Article shall not apply to any person holding the office of President when this Article was proposed by the Congress, and shall not prevent any person who may be holding the office of President, or acting as President, during the term within which this Article becomes operative from holding the office of President or acting as President during the remainder of such term.

Section. 2. This article shall be inoperative unless it shall have been ratified as an amendment to the Constitution by the legislatures of three-fourths of the several States within seven years from the date of its submission to the States by the Congress.

Amendment XXIII

Section. 1. The District constituting the seat of Government of the United States shall appoint in such manner as the Congress may direct:

A number of electors of President and Vice President equal to the whole number of Senators and Representatives in Congress to which the District would be entitled if it were a State, but in no event more than the least populous State; they shall be in addition to those appointed by the States, but they shall be considered, for the purposes of the election of President and Vice President, to be electors appointed by a State; and they shall meet in the District and perform such duties as provided by the twelfth article of amendment.

Section. 2. The Congress shall have power to enforce this article by appropriate legislation.

Amendment XXIV

Section. 1. The right of citizens of the United States to vote in any primary or other election for President or Vice President, for electors for President or Vice President, or for Senator or Representative in Congress, shall not be denied or abridged by the United States or any State by reason of failure to pay any poll tax or other tax.

Section. 2. The Congress shall have power to enforce this article by appropriate legislation.

Amendment XXV

Section. 1. In case of the removal of the President from office or of his death or resignation, the Vice President shall become President.

Section. 2. Whenever there is a vacancy in the office of the Vice President, the President shall nominate a Vice President who shall take office upon confirmation by a majority vote of both Houses of Congress.

Section. 3. Whenever the President transmits to the President pro tempore of the Senate and the Speaker of the House of Representatives his written declaration that he is unable to discharge the powers and duties of his office, and until he transmits to them a written declaration to the contrary, such powers and duties shall be discharged by the Vice President as Acting President.

Section. 4. Whenever the Vice President and a majority of either the principal officers of the executive departments or of such other body as Congress may by law provide, transmit to the President pro tempore of the Senate and the Speaker of the House of Representatives their written declaration that the President is unable to discharge the powers and duties of his office, the Vice President shall immediately assume the powers and duties of the office as Acting President.

Thereafter, when the President transmits to the President pro tempore of the Senate and the Speaker of the House of Representatives his written declaration that no inability exists, he shall resume the powers and duties of his office unless the Vice President and a majority of either the principal officers of the executive department or of such other body as Congress may by law provide, transmit within four days to the President pro tempore of the Senate and the Speaker of the House of Representatives their written declaration that the President is unable to discharge the powers and duties of his office. Thereupon Congress shall decide the issue, assembling within forty-eight hours for that purpose if not in session. If the Congress, within twenty-one days after receipt of the latter written declaration, or, if Congress is not in session, within twenty-one days after Congress is required to assemble, determines by two-thirds vote of both Houses that the President is unable to discharge the powers and duties of his office, the Vice President shall continue to discharge the same as Acting President; otherwise, the President shall resume the powers and duties of his office.

Amendment XXVI

Section. 1. The right of citizens of the United States, who are eighteen years of age or older, to vote shall not be denied or abridged by the United States or by any State on account of age.

Section. 2. The Congress shall have power to enforce this article by appropriate legislation.

Amendment XXVII

No law, varying the compensation for the services of the Senators and Representatives, shall take effect, until an election of Representatives shall have intervened.

Appendix III

For Further Reading

With few exceptions, the quotes in this book were drawn from the American founding period, that swirling maelstrom of ideas that was the American Revolution. And the vast majority of quotes were drawn from the writings of John Adams, who was at the time, and may still be, the preeminent expert on the science of government, both ancient and modern.

> *A Defence of the Constitutions of Government of the United States,* by John Adams (3 Volumes)
>
> *The Political Writings of John Adams,* Edited by George Carey
>
> *The Portable John Adams,* Edited by John Patrick Diggins
>
> *John Adams & The Spirit of Liberty,* by C. Bradley Thompson

The Federalist Papers, by Alexander Hamilton, James Madison and John Jay

The Anti-Federalist Papers and Constitutional Convention Debates

Miracle at Philadelphia, by Catherine Drinker Bowen

E Pluribus Unum, by Forrest McDonald

Novus Ordo Seclorum, by Forrest McDonald

Common Sense, by Thomas Paine

A Familiar Exposition of the Constitution of the United States, by Joseph Story

— A frequent recurrence to the fundamental principles of the constitution, and a constant adherence to those of piety, justice, moderation, temperance, industry, and frugality, are absolutely necessary to preserve the advantages of liberty, and to maintain a free government.[1]

NOTES

Epigraph
1. John Adams, *Notes for an Oration at Braintree* (1772).

Chapter 1
1. John Adams, *The Works of John Adams, Volume IV* (Little, Brown & Co., 1851), p. 194.
2. Alexander Hamilton, James Madison and John Jay, *The Federalist Papers* (Bantam, 1982), #39, p. 190.
3. Roger Sherman to John Adams, July 20, 1789, *The Works of John Adams, Volume VI* (Little, Brown & Co., 1851), p. 437.
4. John Adams, *The Works of John Adams, Volume V* (Little, Brown & Co., 1851), pp. 453-454.
5. Ibid, p. 453.
6. Cicero, *On the Commonwealth I, xxv, 39. Ed.; The Political Writings of John Adams* (Regnery Publishing, 2000), p. 121.
7. John Adams, *The Works of John Adams, Volume IV* (Little, Brown & Co., 1851), p. 401.
8. Ibid, p. 295.
9. John Adams to Roger Sherman, July 17, 1789, *The Works of John Adams, Volume VI* (Little, Brown & Co., 1851), p. 428.
10. John Adams, *The Works of John Adams, Volume VI* (Little, Brown & Co., 1851), p. 170.
11. *The Annals of America, Volume One* (Encyclopaedia Britannica, Inc., 1968), p. 40.
12. *The Mayflower Compact* (1620); George Grant, *The Patriot's Handbook* (Cumberland House Publishing, Inc., 1996), p. 21.

13. John Adams, *The Works of John Adams, Volume IV* (Little, Brown & Co., 1851), p. 295.

Chapter 2

1. Alexander Hamilton, James Madison and John Jay, *The Federalist Papers*, #10, (Bantam, 1982), p. 262.
2. John Adams to John Taylor, *The Works of John Adams, Volume VI* (Little, Brown & Co., 1851), p. 470.
3. John Adams, *The Works of John Adams, Volume IV* (Little, Brown & Co., 1851), p. 420.
4. John Adams to John Taylor, April 15, 1814, *The Works of John Adams, Volume VI* (Little, Brown & Co., 1851), p. 448.
5. *The Anti-Federalist Papers and the Constitutional Convention Debates*, (Mentor, 1986), p. 276.
6. John Adams, *The Works of John Adams, Volume VI* (Little, Brown & Co., 1851), pp. 6-7.
7. John Adams, *The Works of John Adams, Volume IV* (Little, Brown & Co., 1851), p. 301.
8. Ibid, p. 426.
9. John Adams, *The Works of John Adams, Volume V* (Little, Brown & Co., 1851), p. 456.
10. John Adams, *The Works of John Adams, Volume IV* (Little, Brown & Co., 1851), pp. 426-427.
11. Alexander Hamilton, James Madison and John Jay, *The Federalist Papers*, #10, (Bantam, 1982), p. 46.
12. Ibid, p. 63.
13. John Adams, *The Works of John Adams, Volume IV* (Little, Brown & Co., 1851), p. 301.
14. Ibid, p. 473.
15. Ibid, p. 416.
16. Ibid, p. 443.

17. John Quincy Adams, *The Jubilee of the Constitution, A Discourse* (1839).
18. Alexander Hamilton, James Madison and John Jay *The Federalist Papers,* #10, (Bantam, 1982), p. 46.
19. Fisher Ames, *Speech to the Massachusetts Convention* (1788).
20. John Adams, *The Works of John Adams, Volume VI* (Little, Brown & Co., 1851), p. 484.
21. John Adams, *An Essay on Man's Lust for Power* (1763).
22. John Adams, *The Works of John Adams, Volume IV* (Little, Brown & Co., 1851), p. 406.

Chapter 3

1. John Adams, *The Works of John Adams, Volume IV* (Little, Brown & Co., 1851), p. 401.
2. *The Anti-Federalist Papers and the Constitutional Convention Debates,* (Mentor, 1986), p. 276.
3. Alexander Hamilton, *A Farmer, Refuted* (1775)
4. Ibid
5. *The Anti-Federalist Papers and the Constitutional Convention Debates,* (Mentor, 1986), p. 276.
6. John Adams, *Journal* (1772)
7. John Adams, *The Works of John Adams, Volume IV* (Little, Brown & Co., 1851), p. 468.
8. Ibid, p. 359.
9. John Adams, *The Political Writings of John Adams* (Regnery Publishing, 2000), p. 505.
10. John Adams, *The Works of John Adams, Volume IV* (Little, Brown & Co., 1851), p. 466.
11. Alexander Hamilton, *A Farmer, Refuted* (1775)
12. John Adams, *The Political Writings of John Adams* (Regnery Publishing, 2000), p. 506.
13. *Maryland Declaration of Rights* (1776)

14. John Adams, *The Works of John Adams, Volume V* (Little, Brown & Co., 1851), p. 37.
15. John Adams to Roger Sherman, *The Works of John Adams, Volume VI* (Little, Brown & Co., 1851), p. 428.
16. John Adams, *Inaugural Addresses of the Presidents of the United States* (Government Printing Office, 1989), p. 9.

Chapter 4

1. Oscar S. Straus, *Origin of Republican Form of Government* (G.P. Putnam's Sons, 1885), p. 79.
2. John Adams, *The Works of John Adams, Volume VI* (Little, Brown & Co., 1851), p. 217.
3. John Adams, *The Works of John Adams, Volume IV* (Little, Brown & Co., 1851), p. 587.
4. Ibid, p. 297.
5. Ibid, p. 587.
6. Ibid, p. 445.
7. Ibid, p. 383.
8. John Adams, *The Works of John Adams, Volume VI* (Little, Brown & Co., 1851), p. 124.
9. John Adams, *The Works of John Adams, Volume IV* (Little, Brown & Co., 1851), p. 385.
10. Ibid, p. 285.
11. John Adams, *The Works of John Adams, Volume V* (Little, Brown & Co., 1851), pp. 5-6.
12. Ibid, p. 287.
13. Ibid, p. 380.
14. John Adams, *The Works of John Adams, Volume VI* (Little, Brown & Co., 1851), p. 44.
15. Alexander Hamilton, James Madison and John Jay *The Federalist Papers*, #51, (Bantam, 1982), p. 262.
16. *Constitution of the United States* (1787), Article I, Section 7.

17. John Adams, *The Works of John Adams*, Volume IV (Little, Brown & Co., 1851), p. 470.
18. Ibid, p. 447.
19. *Constitution of the United States* (1787), Article I, Section 7.
20. John Adams, *The Works of John Adams*, Volume IV (Little, Brown & Co., 1851), p. 491.
21. Oscar S. Straus, *Origin of Republican Form of Government* (G.P. Putnam's Sons, 1885), p. xxxiv; John Adams, *The Works of John Adams*, Volume IV (Little, Brown & Co., 1851), p. 421.
22. Oscar S. Straus, *Origin of Republican Form of Government* (G.P. Putnam's Sons, 1885), p. xxxiv.
23. John Adams, *The Works of John Adams*, Volume IV (Little, Brown & Co., 1851), p. 435.
24. John Adams, *The Works of John Adams*, Volume V (Little, Brown & Co., 1851), pp. 9-10.
25. John Adams, *The Works of John Adams*, Volume IV (Little, Brown & Co., 1851), p. 370.

Chapter 5

1. John Adams, *The Works of John Adams*, Volume IV (Little, Brown & Co., 1851), p. 579.
2. John Adams to Richard Henry Lee, November 15, 1775, *The Political Writings of John Adams* (Regnery Publishing, 2000), p. 643
3. John Adams, *The Works of John Adams*, Volume IV (Little, Brown & Co., 1851), p. 400.
4. John Adams, *The Works of John Adams*, Volume VI (Little, Brown & Co., 1851), p. 114.
5. Alexander Hamilton, James Madison and John Jay *The Federalist Papers*, #51, (Bantam, 1982), p. 262.
6. John Adams, *The Works of John Adams*, Volume IV (Little, Brown & Co., 1851), p. 462.

7. Ibid, p. 581.
8. John Adams, *The Works of John Adams, Volume VI* (Little, Brown & Co., 1851), p. 172.
9. John Adams, *The Works of John Adams, Volume IV* (Little, Brown & Co., 1851), p. 290.
10. John Adams, *The Works of John Adams, Volume VI* (Little, Brown & Co., 1851), p. 172.
11. John Adams, *The Works of John Adams, Volume IV* (Little, Brown & Co., 1851), p. 290.
12. Ibid, p. 400.
13. John Adams, *The Works of John Adams, Volume IV* (Little, Brown & Co., 1851), p. 424.
14. Alexander Hamilton, James Madison and John Jay *The Federalist Papers*, #51, (Bantam, 1982), p. 394.
15. Ibid, p. 244.
16. John Adams, *The Works of John Adams, Volume IV* (Little, Brown & Co., 1851), p. 424.
17. John Adams, *The Works of John Adams, Volume VI* (Little, Brown & Co., 1851), p. 189.
18. John Adams to John Taylor, *The Political Writings of John Adams* (Regnery Publishing, 2000), p. 410.
19. John Adams, *The Political Writings of John Adams* (Regnery Publishing, 2000), p. 510.

Chapter 6

1. John Adams, *The Works of John Adams, Volume VI* (Little, Brown & Co., 1851), p. 474.
2. John Adams, *The Political Writings of John Adams* (Regnery Publishing, 2000), p. 390.
3. John Adams, *The Works of John Adams, Volume VI* (Little, Brown & Co., 1851), p. 469.

4. John Adams, *The Political Writings of John Adams* (Regnery Publishing, 2000), pp. 499-500.
5. John Adams, *The Works of John Adams, Volume IV* (Little, Brown & Co., 1851), p. 405.
6. Ibid, p. 410.
7. Ibid, p. 408.
8. Ibid, p. 403.
9. John Adams, *Notes for an Oration at Braintree* (1772).
10. John Adams, *The Political Writings of John Adams* (Regnery Publishing, 2000), p. 499.
11. Ibid, p. 500.
12. John Adams, *The Works of John Adams, Volume IV* (Little, Brown & Co., 1851), p. 409.
13. Alexander Hamilton, *A Farmer, Refuted* (1775)
14. John Adams, *The Works of John Adams, Volume IV* (Little, Brown & Co., 1851), p. 408.
15. Ibid, p. 462.
16. Ibid, pp. 557-558.
17. Ibid, p. 567.
18. John Adams, *The Works of John Adams, Volume VI* (Little, Brown & Co., 1851), p. 468.
19. Ibid, p. 50.
20. John Adams, *The Works of John Adams, Volume IV* (Little, Brown & Co., 1851), pp. 491-492.
21. John Adams, *The Works of John Adams, Volume VI* (Little, Brown & Co., 1851), p. 44.
22. John Adams, *The Political Writings of John Adams* (Regnery Publishing, 2000), p. 505.
23. John Adams, *The Works of John Adams, Volume VI* (Little, Brown & Co., 1851), p. 415.

24. John Adams, *The Works of John Adams, Volume IV* (Little, Brown & Co., 1851), p. 284.
25. Ibid, p. 318.
26. Alexander Hamilton, *A Farmer, Refuted* (1775).
27. John Adams to Abigail Adams, July 7, 1775.
28. John Adams, *The Works of John Adams, Volume III* (Little, Brown & Co., 1851), pp. 456-457.
29. Ibid, p. 448.
30. John Adams, *The Works of John Adams, Volume VI* (Little, Brown & Co., 1851), p. 219.
31. Ibid, p. 458.
32. John Adams, *The Works of John Adams, Volume IV* (Little, Brown & Co., 1851), p. 424.
33. John Adams, *The Works of John Adams, Volume VI* (Little, Brown & Co., 1851), p. 88.
34. John Adams, *The Works of John Adams, Volume IV* (Little, Brown & Co., 1851), p. 293.

Appendix I
1. Joseph J. Ellis, *Passionate Sage* (W. W. Norton & Company, 1994), p. 29.

Appendix III
1. John Adams, *The Works of John Adams, Volume IV* (Little, Brown & Co., 1851), p. 227.

ABOUT THE AUTHOR

Will Butts was born in Boston, and is a graduate of Eastern Nazarene College. Interested in history from a very early age, he intended to teach, but instead was drawn into the worlds of banking and business. *This Republic* is Will's first book and reflects his real passion. Will works as an accountant and lives in Quincy, Massachusetts, City of Presidents.

Will can be contacted via the publisher, libertyslampbooks.com.

www.ingramcontent.com/pod-product-compliance
Lightning Source LLC
Chambersburg PA
CBHW031424290426
44110CB00011B/516